MW01291814

The Way of the Linguist

A Language Learning Odyssey

by

Steve Kaufmann

authorHOUSE™

1663 LIBERTY DRIVE, SUITE 200
BLOOMINGTON, INDIANA 47403
(800) 839-8640
WWW.AUTHORHOUSE.COM

This book is a work of non-fiction. Unless otherwise noted, the author and the publisher make no explicit guarantees as to the accuracy of the information contained in this book and in some cases, names of people and places have been altered to protect their privacy.

© 2005 Steve Kaufmann. All Rights Reserved.

No part of this book may be reproduced, stored in a retrieval system, or transmitted by any means without the written permission of the author.

First published by AuthorHouse 11/21/05

ISBN: 1-4208-7329-6 (sc)

Library of Congress Control Number: 2005906876

Printed in the United States of America
Bloomington, Indiana

This book is printed on acid-free paper.

The Linguist is a trademark of Steve Kaufmann

This book, or parts thereof, may not be reproduced in any form without permission in writing from Steve Kaufmann, except by a reviewer, who may quote brief passages in a review.

First edition July 2003
Printed in Canada

Table of Contents

Zhuangzi's Crooked Tree

Huizi said to Zhuangzi, "This old tree is so crooked and rough that it is useless for lumber. In the same way, your teachings have no practical use."

Zhuangzi replied, "This tree may be useless as lumber, but you could rest in the gentle shade of its big branches or admire its rustic character. It only seems useless to you because you want to turn it into something else and don't know how to appreciate it for what it is. My teachings are like this."

Zhuangzi, the Taoist philosopher, lived in China over 2,300 years ago. He taught the Tao, or way, an approach to life based on effortlessness and harmony with one's nature.   He was down to earth and had a tongue in cheek sense of humour. He made fun of ritual, dogma, and pretentious moralizing. His epigrams and parables praised those who achieved mastery through constant practice of a skill, following their own inclinations. He scorned complicated explanations and theories.

Zhuangzi's famous story about the crooked tree appeals to me for many reasons. Being in the forest industry, I know that a crooked tree is not suitable for making standard commodity lumber products, but it can make high quality decorative products which feature its natural beauty and individuality.

Such a tree has grown to a ripe old age by adapting itself to its environment. Whereas the trees in the industrial forest are straight and look alike, the crooked tree grew alone, or with a mixture of other trees of different ages and species. This kind of tree will resist wind and disease better than the more uniform trees of the plantation forest.

People who follow their natures and pursue their own path to language learning will be happier and more successful than learners who try meet goals set for them by others. A true language learner must be like the crooked tree of Zhuangzi, not seeking perfection of form, but prospering by taking advantage of surrounding resources. Think of the crooked tree. Please read this book to learn how to take advantage of the abundant language resources and opportunities for communication that surround you. And most of all, just enjoy yourself!

Respect gods before demi-gods, heroes
before men, and first among men your parents,
but respect yourself most of all.
-Pythagoras, 6th century BC

INTRODUCTION

Are You a Linguist?

As I see it, everyone is a potential linguist. By that, I mean that everyone can be fluent in another language. You do not have to be an intellectual or an academic. After all, a linguist is defined by the Concise Oxford Dictionary in very simple terms:

Linguist: n. Person skilled in foreign languages.

Even speaking one foreign language qualifies a person as a linguist. To become a linguist is a matter of choice, and requires a certain state of mind. A linguist enjoys foreign languages and appreciates the different ways that ideas are organized and expressed in different cultures. A linguist is at ease with people of another language and confident when learning new languages. To a linguist, learning a new language is a natural and enjoyable thing to do.

The first step towards becoming a linguist, towards learning a second language, is to realize that success depends not on the teacher, but on the learner. Each learner must discover the language gradually in his or her own way. The teacher can only stimulate and inspire. Enrolling in a language school or taking a course will not ensure fluency. If the learner does not accept this simple fact, time and money spent on language programs will be wasted. Language schools and language learning systems may teach, but only the learner can learn.

Growing up in the English-speaking area of Montreal, a predominantly French-speaking city, I remember that until the age of seventeen, I could not maintain a conversation in French. I was not interested in learning another language, although I had been taught French at school from the second grade and was surrounded by the French language. Yet today, I can speak nine languages and have derived immense satisfaction and reward from being able to speak Mandarin Chinese, French, Japanese, Spanish, German, Swedish, Cantonese and Italian.

In order to try to understand why this happened, I began writing down the history of my own language learning. I realized that it was only when I had a genuine desire to communicate or learn something meaningful in a new language that I was able to learn. When the subject of study was based on the details of the language itself, I resisted. When teachers tried to impose abstract principles of grammar and then test me on them, I remained passive. But once I decided that I needed the language to connect with real people or a new culture, I would throw myself into the study of the language with passion and commitment. And I needed passion, because for me language learning was very hard work.

It was while learning Cantonese at the age of fifty-five that I became aware that language learning had become dramatically easier and more exciting. Modern electronic technology has created opportunities for language enjoyment that did not exist when I was learning. The production of high quality audio books in CD and MP3 format is expanding rapidly. MP3 technology enables high quality, entertaining, and informative sound files to be shared on the Internet. We do not know just how far this new medium, so called "podcasting", will change the way we share information in many languages. In fact, today the Internet provides a vast range of interesting and authentic second language content for learners to choose from, in both audio and electronic text formats. With the text in electronic format the reader can access instant dictionary software and create personal databases of new words and phrases that are linked to meaningful contexts, not learner language. A wealth of foreign language books and magazines that used to be too difficult for a language learner are suddenly accessible and can serve as the core content for learning. What is more, the Internet itself can serve as the hub for a community of learners and native speakers.

As I wrote the story of my own language learning, I decided to develop a new approach to language learning based on the principles that worked for me, but taking advantage of modern technology to ensure that a new generation of language learners can learn more easily than I did. Under my direction, a small group of language learners and computer programmers immediately started developing these ideas into a comprehensive new language learning system. The more we worked on this project, the more excited we became about our potential to increase the number of real linguists worldwide, by making language learning affordable, enjoyable and effective.

The word "globalization" is commonly used to describe the intensity of international exchange that we are experiencing today. Some people declare themselves in favour of globalization, and others are against it. To me, globalization is an irresistible trend, an inevitable direction of the evolution of our world. It is somewhat pointless to be "for" or "against" something that is inevitable. It is more useful to invest time and energy in being able to enjoy and profit from globalization by becoming a linguist.

I do not think globalization needs to lead to the domination of one language, such as English. Rather, I see it as an opportunity for all people, including English speakers, to become better acquainted with other cultures. Paradoxically, now that the world seems a much smaller place, we are seeing a general renewal of interest in regional languages and identities. There is an increasing demand for effective methods of language learning, not only for dominant languages like English, but also for languages spoken by fewer people. The cost of preparing learning materials for these languages and the effort needed to learn them can be dramatically reduced. Modern technology can make the natural living language itself a lively and effective learning resource.

I am confident that this book and the methods described in it can contribute towards helping people to become linguists.

About Learning English

English is well established as the most useful world language. The largest demand for second language instruction in the world is for English. Whether we like it or not, English dominates in business, science, travel and popular culture, not to mention the Internet. English is a rather clumsy language, combining the influences of Old English, Latin, Norman French and natural evolution. As a result, English has all kinds of inconsistencies of grammar and spelling to frustrate the learner. Yet English dominates, whereas artificial international languages like Esperanto have never had any following.

Two thousand years ago, or even five hundred years ago, it would have seemed ridiculous to suppose that the language spoken on a small damp North Atlantic island would one day be the world's most widely used language. Certainly, Chinese, Latin, Greek, Arabic, or even Mongolian would, at various times in history, have seemed more likely candidates. Who knows what languages will be spoken in another five hundred years? As Spencer Wells explains in *The Journey of Man, A Genetic Odyssey* (Princeton University Press) "[Although] Sogdian was once the lingua franca of the Silk Road – in much the same way that English is the language of commerce today, by the twentieth century all dialects were extinct but one."

If you are not a native speaker of English, then I encourage you to read this book in English. This may be the first book that you read in English, but you can do it. Perhaps most of the English content you have read up until now has consisted of short texts or articles. Perhaps the thought of reading a whole book in English is intimidating to you. It should not be.

This book contains over 4,000 of the most common English words. This book is printed on paper, the most comfortable and intimate format. Books are portable and convenient. But I have also recorded the contents on a CD so that you can hear the language and allow it to stimulate those neural networks in your brain which respond to spoken language. Finally, the book is available in electronic format so you can look up words using dictionary software and take advantage of a host of other interactive functions of electronic text.

I recommend you read this book in your own language first to become familiar with the contents and principles of language learning. But then please listen to the audio version in English, segment by segment, and read the corresponding electronic texts to make sure you understand what you are listening to. From the electronic texts you can easily look up and save new words and phrases to personalized lists for regular review. In so doing you will start to develop the habit of learning in a self-directed and integrated manner.

About this Book

This book is divided into three sections that may be read in any order.

- **A LANGUAGE ADVENTURE** describes my experience in acquiring eight languages in a variety of environments and at different stages of my life. I include personal observations reflecting my curiosity about culture and history. These observations may seem unrelated to language learning, but they are not. A linguist needs to be a curious adventurer.

- **THE ATTITUDE OF A LINGUIST** describes the attitudes that are essential to successful language study. More than any other factor, your attitude will determine your success in language learning. The description of these attitudes will reinforce conclusions that the reader will make in reading the autobiographical section.

- **HOW TO LEARN LANGUAGES** is about the nuts and bolts of how to learn languages. You may wish to read this section first; however, you should still read the whole book to fully understand what is required to become a linguist.

All languages can be enjoyable to learn, if you recognize that perfection is not a reasonable goal. You are constantly learning and improving in the new language as you use it. Therefore, as early as possible, the learning process should be built around genuine and enjoyable communication. If you enjoy learning and communicating in a new language and if you are committed to improving , this book can help you achieve your goals.

Happy the man who, like Ulysses, has made a fine voyage,
or has won the Golden Fleece,
and then returns, experienced and knowledgeable,
to spend the rest of his life among his family!
– **Joachim du Bellay (1522-60), French poet**

A LANGUAGE ADVENTURE

The Start of the Journey

Language learning is a form of travel, a journey of discovery. I started traveling when I was very young and have always found travel stimulating. A true linguist needs to be adventurous and to overcome the fear of the unknown. To illustrate this, let me tell you my story.

I was born in Sweden in 1945 and emigrated to Montreal, Canada as a five year old with my parents and older brother Tom. My memories begin in Canada. I have no recollection of having spoken any language other than English as a child, although I know that I spoke Swedish first. It is possible that having to learn a second language as a child helped me to become a better language learner as an adult. However, I know other people who emigrated to Canada as children and did not become linguists. I also know people who were born in Canada and grew up only in English but have become excellent linguists. I attribute my success in language learning to a spirit of adventure and a willingness to study with a great deal of intensity. I believe others can do the same if they are prepared to embark on the exciting journey of language discovery.

One of my earliest memories of Montreal is an incident in 1952. A group of us six-year-olds had a favorite hiding place for our baseball bat. After school we always retrieved the bat and played baseball. One day the bat was gone. Immediately we deduced that it was the new boy from Estonia who had stolen the bat. It was obvious to us that it was him. He did not speak English well. He was the outsider. The only problem was that he had not taken the bat. He probably did not even know what a baseball bat was used for. In the end, it was all settled amicably. I guess that I, after one year in Canada, was already accepted into the "in group". Thereafter the boy from Estonia was, too. This incident has always remained with me as an example of how people can unthinkingly stick together and resist the participation of an outsider.

But acceptance is a two way street. Insiders may initially resist a newcomer, but it is also up to the outsider to be adventurous and make the effort to be accepted. In most cases, when I have overcome my apprehensions and made the effort to be accepted by a different language group, the response has been more welcoming than I could have imagined. I think there are far more examples of newcomers hesitating or not making the effort to join, and thereby losing opportunities, than of newcomers being rejected. A language learner is by definition an outsider, coming from a different language group. You must take risks in order to be accepted. This is a major principle of language learning: be adventurous. It worked for me, and French was my first language adventure.

Two Solitudes in Montreal

The life of an English speaking Montrealer growing up in the Western part of the city in the 1950s was not very different from the life of English speaking North Americans elsewhere on the continent. To show their commitment to our new homeland, my parents decided that they would speak only English with my brother and me. I went to English school, had only English friends, listened to English radio and watched English television. As a result, by the time I turned seventeen in 1962, I had only a very limited ability to express myself in French.

Of course we had French at school. I passed all my French classes with good marks, but I could not function in French in the real world. Most of the one million English speaking Montrealers of that day were not interested in communicating with their two million French speaking fellow citizens in French. English was the language of business and the dominant language of the North American continent. I was no exception to this general attitude. We were hardly aware of the larger French speaking city surrounding us. This all seems extraordinary now, but in those days it was quite accurate to talk of "two solitudes" in Montreal.

I should point out that the reality of Montreal has changed in the last forty years. English speaking Montrealers are now among the most bilingual people in Canada. French has been made important and meaningful to them because of political changes in the province of Quebec. As a result, Montreal is a vibrant city with a unique atmosphere of its own.

There is an important point here. Obviously it is an advantage for a language learner to live in an environment where the second language is spoken. However, this does not guarantee language acquisition. You must have a positive attitude towards the language and culture you are trying to learn. You cannot learn to communicate if you rely on a classroom where the focus is on trying to pass tests. Only a genuine desire to communicate with another culture can ensure language learning success.

In 1961, when I was sixteen, I spent a summer visiting with my uncle Fritz in Stockholm. My mother had died in May of that year. Fritz was her brother and they had been especially close, even though they lived far apart from each other. Spending time with him was of comfort to me in dealing with the loss of my mother. My uncle, and his wife Lore, became very close to me, almost like parents. When I first arrived I spoke no Swedish, much to the disappointment of my young cousin, Tommy, who was six years old at the time. In the car returning from picking me up at lStockhom Airport, he cried out of frustration at not being able to communicate with his older cousin from Canada. One day he would become fluent in English, and I would become fluent in Swedish. But that was later.

Fritz found me a job for one month working in a department store warehouse. There, I picked up some Swedish from my co-workers. I was later to work hard to develop my Swedish vocabulary in order to be able to use it socially and professionally. But learning Swedish was not my main concern that summer. I spent hours in conversation with Fritz, in English, learning details about life in the small town of Prostiov, Czechoslovakia, where my parents and Fritz had grown up.

My parents were born in what was then the Austro-Hungarian Empire and belonged to a Jewish community which was culturally and linguistically German. The social life of the Jewish community centred around the local coffee house called Deutches Haus or German House. When my parents were children, Goethe, Schiller and Beethoven were the cultural gods and Vienna was the centre of the universe. After the establishment of an independent Czechoslovakian state, my parents were sent to Czech school, and the composers Dvorak, Smetana and the political leaders Benes and Masaryk entered their pantheon. My parents thus grew up speaking German and Czech and also learned English and French. This was normal for their time and place. But for me, a generation later, growing up in North America, it was quite normal to speak only English. This would change for me.

Sweden is where my parents spent the first twelve years of their marriage, from 1939 to 1951, and where my brother and I were born. My father, a paint chemist, had obtained a job as production manager at a varnish factory in Lidingo, a pleasant suburb of Stockholm. Thanks to Sweden, my parents escaped the fate that awaited the Jewish community of Czechoslovakia after the German invasion of 1939. My uncle Fritz, who spent the war with the British Army, was able to join my parents in Sweden in 1946. I have good reasons to have special feelings of affection for Sweden. But it has been my ability to speak Swedish well, which I developed later, that has made my relationship with Sweden and Swedish people especially rewarding and enjoyable.

My father emigrated from Sweden to Canada because he was concerned that the Soviet Union would take over much of Europe. As is often the case with immigrants, he was unable to find work in his profession in Canada. Instead, he started a small business importing clothing from Europe. At the end of my summer in Sweden I accompanied my father on part of his business trip to Italy and France before returning to Canada.

 We flew from Stockholm to Milan and from there went by train and small boat to spend a weekend at a beautiful little hotel on Lake Como. I then followed my father to Florence where he had suppliers to meet. This busy Renaissance city surrounded by hillsides of villas and tall elegant cypress trees seemed to me like a scene out of a history book. We flew on to Nice. There, the night before returning home, I ate an evening meal with my father at a waterfront restaurant on the French Riviera. Lights were strung along the jagged Mediterranean coastline for as far as the eye could see in both directions. It was as if the lights were enticing me on to explore just one more bay, just one more town. I returned to Montreal a changed person. The sudden awareness of a vast exciting world to discover was an enlightenment for me.

"Enlightenment is the triumph of the human being over his self-imposed immaturity."
(Immanuel Kant) 1783

That fall, at the age of seventeen, I entered McGill University. One of my courses was on French civilization, taught by a sarcastic but stimulating professor by the name of Maurice Rabotin. He changed my life. I suddenly became interested in French literature and theatre. With that came an interest in French singers, French food and the *ambiance* of French culture. I was suddenly dealing with the real language and real people. Our teacher was really French, not an English speaking person teaching French, as in high school. The texts we read were real books, not French textbooks specially prepared for language learners.

Perhaps because it was new to me, French culture seemed more free and spontaneous than the English speaking North American culture I had grown up with. It was an exotic new world. I suddenly wanted to learn French. I went to French theatre, made French speaking friends and started reading the French newspapers and listening to French radio. I became aware of the issues that concerned my French speaking fellow citizens and, through attending meetings and discussions, my French language skills improved naturally. I also gained an understanding of the aspirations and grievances of the French speaking Quebeckers.

The six million or so French speaking Quebeckers, descendants of a few tens of thousands of French settlers in the 17th century, had developed into a conservative and inward looking society as a means of self-protection against the growing influence of English speaking North America. The French language and the Catholic religion were the pillars of their identity.

Their conservative attitudes towards education and modern society had left them at a disadvantage in competing with English speaking Canadians, even within their own province of Quebec. Of course, the English speaking minority in Quebec was only too glad to take advantage of this weakness to dominate in all areas of economic activity. Even though they controlled the politics, the French speakers were second class citizens in their own home.

A major sore point was the low status of the French language. Starting in 1960, a growing nationalist movement based on French language rights and a constructive program of secularization, modernization and political activism brought about significant change in the province. Most of this change has been positive, even if there are examples of excess in defense of the French language. The French speaking society of Canada, and Quebec in particular, has its own specific characteristics. Efforts to preserve its cultural identity are justified. New immigrants are joining this French language community and bringing fresh influences as the nature of that society continues to evolve, just as immigrants are joining and redefining English Canada.

French was the first language I started to study seriously. I was not sure of just how fluent I could become. I cannot say that I was confident that I could succeed in speaking almost like a native speaker. That confidence would come later. Much later, when I started to learn other languages, I always had the confidence that I could learn to be as fluent as I wanted. Once you have mastered one new language you gain the confidence necessary to master other languages. You build up your confidence as you learn.

I became fluent in French by giving up the traditional approach of trying to perfect my grammar. Perfection did not matter anymore, only communicating did. I no longer disliked language learning. I read what I liked even if I did not understand all of it. I spoke with people who interested me, struggling to understand and to make myself understood. I was mostly interested in connecting with the culture. I also started to appreciate the sound and structure of the new language. When you move from an attitude of resisting the strangeness of a language to an attitude of appreciating its unique ways of expression and turns of phrase, you are on your way to becoming a linguist.

I Take Charge of My Learning

I took charge of my learning, and stopped relying on my teachers. The teacher was only one of many resources available to me in a city like Montreal. All of a sudden, with no tests, no questions from teachers, and no grammar drills, my French skills took a great leap forward! I had achieved my first language breakthrough. I could feel the improvements in fluency, comprehension and pronunciation. This made language learning exciting. I was speaking and listening to French in situations that interested me. I spoke to myself in French, imitating proper pronunciation as much as I could. Even when I did not understand what was said or had trouble expressing myself, it did not frustrate me. I was committed and I was enjoying the experience of communicating. There was no turning back. By taking my language learning out of the classroom, I had made it real.

I have held onto this central principle: learning done in real situations is always far superior to artificial contexts such as exercises, drills, or material specially designed for learners. Time spent in genuine and interesting conversation is a better learning environment than the formal classroom. I also discovered another important principle of language learning: the learner has to be in charge, seeking out the language, the people, the content. As the learner, I have to discover the words and the phrases that I am going to need. All too often it is the teacher or textbooks who decide which words you should learn. These words have no importance, and as a consequence are quickly forgotten.

Off to Europe

My Adventure Begins

The success of my efforts in Montreal made me more committed to mastering French and so I decided to go to France. Commitment leads to success and success reinforces commitment.

In June of 1962, I quit my summer construction job and went to the Montreal docks to look for a working trip to Europe. For three days I climbed on board oceangoing freighters, asked to see the Captain and then offered to work in exchange for passage to Europe. On the third day I got lucky. A small German tramp steamer, the *Gerda Schell* out of Flensburg, had lost a sailor in Quebec City and needed a crewman for the return voyage. I was on my way.

Aside from the hard work and constant tossing of the small tramp ship on the North Atlantic, the voyage was an opportunity to experience just how inaccurate cultural stereotypes can be. The crew was half German and half Spanish. Contrary to what I had been conditioned to expect, the supposedly industrious Germans were laid back and often drunk, whereas the supposedly temperamental Spanish were tremendously hard working and serious.

We arrived in London after ten days at sea. I ate as much as possible of the free food on the ship in the hope that I would save money by not having to eat for the next day. In fact, that strategy was not so wise and I ended up feeling ill.

London seemed an oddly exotic place to me, since everyone spoke English and yet it was so different from home. Speaker's Corner in Hyde Park has stuck in my memory, as has the old money system of shillings and pence and quids and bobs and guineas. I also remember that I spent one night sleeping on a sidewalk to get tickets to see Laurence Olivier in Shakespeare's *Othello* but then had trouble staying awake during the performance. I stayed in London for one week and then pressed on for the continent to pursue my language learning adventure.

I took the ferry from Dover in the United Kingdom and arrived in Ostende in Belgium after nightfall. A Flemish Belgian on a motor scooter gave me a lift to the medieval city of Bruges. I was young and ignorant and had not read the history of Flanders during the Middle Ages, nor did I realize that the same kinds of language tensions that existed in Quebec were also burning in Belgium between the Flemish speakers and the French speakers. I would return later to Bruges to explore the well preserved medieval atmosphere of that town. But I was a young man in a hurry then, and the following day I hitchhiked on to France.

The French have a reputation for being rude, but the people I met were friendly and hospitable. Outside of Lille in Northern France, I was picked up by two schoolteachers who allowed me to spend the night in a schoolroom, since this was the period of the summer vacation. Then they invited me out to dinner, where I met some people who drove me to Paris the next day. I can still remember the feeling as we drove down *l'Avenue de la Grande Armée* towards the *Arc de Triomphe*, which I had seen so often in films. I could not believe I was really there.

My French friends invited me to stay two weeks in their modest apartment in the 20th Arrondissement, a working-class district of Paris. I was given a short term job in a travel bureau doing translations. I lived and ate with these people for two delightful weeks, as I explored the city on foot and via the Metro (subway). My new friends included me on picnics to chateaux outside Paris and other social occasions. I was sorry when I finally decided to move on south.

I realized very early in my stay in France that even my less than perfect French enabled me to make friends and deal with people in a relaxed manner. I was neither self-conscious nor concerned about how I sounded, I just enjoyed being able to communicate. Of course, I occasionally met Frenchmen who were not so friendly. It is true that many public employees take a particular delight in saying "Non!" Often if you inquire whether some service is available, you are treated to a litany of rejection: "Ah non, alors là, non, mais sûrement pas, mais cela va pas, non!"

But the secret to survival in a foreign country or culture is to make light of the unpleasant and focus on the positive. My French was far from perfect, and it was sometimes an uneven struggle against the more arrogant and impatient French *fonctionnaires* (officials) and shopkeepers. But today I do not remember too many unpleasant incidents because I did not attach much importance to them. I do remember, however, a case when my lack of French got me into trouble.

At one point in my first year in France I had an American girlfriend whose parents were working in Alicante, Spain. We decided to hitchhike there during the Easter holidays. I brought along a gift, a record by Georges Brassens, a popular French *chansonnier*. Being a converted Francophile, I took great pleasure in listening to his songs even though I did not always understand the words. Unfortunately, I did not realize that his words can be quite spicy, if not outright pornographic. When my hosts listened to the gift that I had brought, they were shocked. I think they were concerned about the kind of company their daughter was keeping.

I stayed in France for three years. My first year was in Grenoble, an industrial city in the French Alps. Unfortunately, I never had the time to ski. If I wasn't studying, I was working. At various times I pressed bales of waste paper and drove a delivery van for a printing shop, was busboy in the Park Hotel, hawked the *France Soir* newspaper in the major squares and cafés of Grenoble, and taught English. I even managed to play hockey for the Grenoble University hockey team. An added attraction of Grenoble was the presence of a large contingent of Swedish girls studying French. I was able to learn a bit more Swedish.

"Sciences Po"

I was lucky enough to get a scholarship from the French government for my second two years and moved to Paris where I entered L'Institut d'Études Politiques (the School of Political Studies). "Sciences Po," as this school is called, is located near St. Germain Cathedral in the heart of the medieval part of Paris, just off the Quartier Latin, or students' quarter. Sciences Po boasts many illustrious alumni, including former Canadian Prime Minister Pierre Trudeau.

The teaching culture at Sciences Po was different from North America. The emphasis was on learning facts and being able to organize them quickly according to a time-honored formula. I still remember when a Law Professor told me that "the form was more important than the content!"

The method for organizing your thoughts at Sciences Po was simple. Whatever you wanted to say had to fit into the following formula: Introduction, Part One, Part Two and Conclusion. It was important that Part One and Part Two were about the same length. Ideally, Part One presented one point of view or Thesis, Part Two presented a contrary position or Antithesis, and the Conclusion presented a resolution or Synthesis. Voilà!

This emphasis on a logical and balanced presentation of information is a useful discipline for communicating in any language. This technique helped me to organize my essays and oral presentations in French, which was, after all, still a foreign language to me. When writing or speaking in a foreign language, it is particularly important to have a basic formula for organizing your thoughts, otherwise it is too easy to just ramble on because you lack control in the new language.

Obviously writing a business report, writing an essay on philosophy and writing an academic paper all require you to organize your information in different ways. You need to be more formal and structured than when you engage in casual conversation. The preferred structure for such writing will even vary from culture to culture. However, whenever I wrote in a foreign language, and French was my first, I felt that the individual sentences I wrote were the same as my spoken language. In my mind I made no distinction between the written and the spoken language, even though there undoubtedly was one. I always tried to make them both as similar as possible. I recommend this approach to all language learners as a way to improve the accuracy of both your written and spoken language.

I do not believe it is helpful to divide a language into categories to be learned as separate skills. Today there are courses offered in business language, academic language, technical language and so forth. To me language is one. To be effective and persuasive in a new language you have to build a solid base of key phrases and words that you can use comfortably in speaking and writing. If you have that base, technical vocabulary is easily acquired. If you can express yourself clearly and logically, you can easily learn to write business reports or academic papers.

The courses at Sciences Po were very stimulating. The most interesting lecturers, such as Jean-Baptiste Duroselle, spoke to overflowing audiences. We were taught plenty of facts and the professors were very definite in their views, often bristling with irony. They were not interested in the ideas of their students. Yet somehow I found this atmosphere more stimulating than the one I had left behind at McGill University. Canadian English speaking intellectual circles are less tolerant of genuine originality than the French. This is particularly the case in today's politically correct age.

The reason for this, I believe, is the deeper tradition of learning and greater intellectual confidence of the French.

The French place importance on being able to express yourself with elegance and precision. The most important exam for students at Sciences Po was the Oral Exam, a spoken essay. Students were given a few minutes to organize a fifteen-minute presentation to a senior panel of professors on a subject selected at random. The students were judged as much on their ability to express their views in a balanced and logical way as on the actual content or information they were able to provide.

There is a tendency today to teach spoken language as different from written language. I disagree with this approach. Effective spoken language is similar to effective written language: clear, simple and elegant. While it is true that native speakers can be a little sloppy in their spoken language, I do not believe that this should be taught as a model to new learners. Slang and excessive colloquialisms do not suit the non-native speaker until he or she is comfortable in the language. Learners should try to speak the way they write. I have always tried to use the same clear sentences and phrases when I speak as when I write in a foreign language. I avoid a too casual spoken style or an overly complicated written style. In this way, regular writing practice can be a great help to learning to speak correctly.

Travel and Culture

The French pride themselves on their logic. Whatever goes against their logic is wrong, and is attacked without pity. For this reason they are sometimes seen as unfriendly or arrogant. To me, however, France was not only a stimulating country but also a very hospitable one. I received a scholarship that enabled me to enjoy my last two years in France. I met kindness and generosity from French people of all walks of life. While hitchhiking in the countryside, I was often invited to meals and to stay at people's homes.

My commitment to the French language and culture helped create bridges with people. I am sure this would not have been possible had I remained a typical Anglophone North American. There are many English speaking North Americans who have been very successful at learning new languages. However, it is more commonly non-English speakers who make the effort to learn English. While this is unavoidable because of the unique international usefulness of English, it is a great loss to those English speakers who never experience the personal enrichment of learning a new language.

I delighted in visiting the countryside, seeing the historic villages and towns, and talking with people in French. As with most countries, France has regional accents. When you speak a foreign language you have to imitate the native speaker to acquire a native speaker accent. In my case, this meant that I spoke with a Parisian accent in Paris, a Southern accent on the Mediterranean, and so forth. This is hard to avoid, at least in the early stages. But it is also a good sign, since it shows that you are listening carefully to the pronunciation of native speakers.

Nevertheless, I have always felt that it is best for a non-native speaker to adopt the most standard form of the language rather than a regional accent. In every country there is a form of the language that is considered the standard. It might be the French spoken in Tours, the Mandarin spoken in Beijing, or the Japanese spoken in Tokyo. It is always amusing to hear a foreigner speak in a regional accent, but the neutral feel of the standard pronunciation is usually the wiser course. Canadian English is such a standard or neutral form of English.

In a similar vein, a language learner is best to stay clear of idioms, slang and swear words. There is a lot of French slang, or *argot* as it is called, that I still do not understand. It does not bother me. I do not usually come across it in my reading, and I am not expected to be able to use it when I speak. Some language learners are in a hurry to use slang expressions before they know how to use them. I think a non-native speaker sounds best speaking in correct standard language.

The history of France is a history of the different people who have created Europe. Some of the earliest examples of human painting and sculpture are located in the caves of Southwestern France, dating back as far as 20,000 years ago. At the time of the Roman conquest over 2,000 years ago, the Celtic Gauls were dominant in France, although there were Greek colonies in the South, various other tribes in the North and the ancient Basques in the Southwest. The Romans brought with them their civilization, and created an engineering infrastructure that still survives in the amphitheaters, roads and aqueducts that tourists can visit today, especially in the South of France. With the Romans came the staples of the Mediterranean culinary tradition: bread, olive oil, and wine.

So France is a melting pot, as most countries are if you go back far enough. This is reflected in the varying myths of origin of the French. Sometimes they emphasize their Gallic ancestry. At other times, the French are proud of their Latin roots and sympathize more with Mediterranean people than with Northern Europeans. Certainly their literature is dominated by references to the Classics of Roman and Greek antiquity. Yet the early heroes of France, including Clovis, Pepin le Bref, Charles Martel, and Charlemagne, were Germanic Franks.

A concern with food and drink is one of the dominant features of modern French culture, and the subject of conversation at all levels of society. The French recognize that elegantly and enthusiastically talking about a subject is a large part of the enjoyment.

Long after my studies in France were over, I had the opportunity to lead a group of Japanese wood industry executives on a tour of wood processing plants in France. I remember on one occasion we arrived at a modern door and window plant near Toulouse. For many minutes our delegation was kept waiting while our French hosts were engaged in an animated discussion. My Japanese tour members sat patiently, but eventually they wanted to know what the argument was all about. I explained that our French hosts were discussing what we were going to have for lunch. I still remember my meal of *salade tiède de gésiers* and *cassoulet*, eaten under the shade of pine trees outside an old Mediterranean chateau. My memory of the factory we visited is less clear.

With French, as with other languages, a familiarity with the food is an important part of learning the culture and the language. Conviviality around a meal table can be the best learning environment. Cicero, the Roman statesman and orator, defined *convivium* as *"to sit down to dinner*

13

with friends because they share one's life." This desire to communicate over food is common to all languages and cultures, and no doubt has an origin in the prehistoric sharing of the hunt. It reinforces a feeling of reciprocity between people. As a poor student, I did not often have the chance to enjoy haute cuisine. However, it was not uncommon when I was hitchhiking in Southern France for truck drivers to share with me a full course lunch, including wine. How they continued driving after that was a bit of a mystery to me. I understand that the control on drinking and driving in France has become more severe in recent years.

Hitchhiking in Europe

I am sure I hitchhiked tens of thousands of miles in those years, criss-crossing Europe from Spain to Sweden to Italy through Germany and all countries in between. There was no better way to explore the history and geography, to meet people and practice languages. Unfortunately hitchhiking is no longer as easy as it used to be.

My accommodations varied a great deal. Mostly I stayed in youth hostels, which were great places to meet up with travelers from other countries. Often I met these same travelers standing on the roads leading out of town with their thumbs out, large rucksacks hidden beside the platane trees, as we all tried to hitch a ride to our next destination.

I have lain awake frozen on a windswept mountain side on the Route Napoleon on my way from the French Alps to the Mediterranean, before being able to warm myself the next day by napping in the gentle sun of the lavender fields of Grasse just before reaching the sea at Nice. I have slept in parks, in ditches, on beaches and in hotels of every description. On two occasions, once in Boeblingen, Germany and once in Perpignan, France, I checked into the local jail, where I was kindly accommodated until the morning. I had not committed a crime, but it was late and raining. The police seemed happy to have the company. I was the only guest in both establishments, which were basic but clean.

My usual routes took me through southern France, the Midi, with its quaint stone villages, dry Mediterranean vegetation, Roman ruins, historical cities like Avignon, Nimes and Arles, and old men playing *boules* on the sandy town squares. The temperature could easily exceed forty degrees Celsius in the summer.

From there I would continue into Franco's Spain, a favorite holiday hitchhiking destination for me in the early 1960s. Spanish vocabulary and grammar is similar to French, since both languages can be considered dialects of Latin. With a little bit of study and reading in Spanish, and daily conversation with the friendly and talkative Spaniards, I was able to bring my Spanish up to an acceptable level. On my first visit to Barcelona, as I climbed aboard a crowded city bus, I was overwhelmed by the friendliness of the people. They helped me on with my rucksack, made sure I knew where the Youth Hostel was located, and then invited me for a drink at the local bar. We all drank out of a communal wine pitcher with a long spout which was held at arm's length so a long stream of wine could flow into your mouth.

> **With my interest in history and adventure, I found Spain to be as fascinating a mixture of peoples and cultures as France. Basques, Celts, Iberians, Greeks, Romans, Visigoths, Arabs, Berbers, Jews, and Gypsies (originally from India), have all contributed their genetic, cultural and linguistic influence.**
>
> **Nowadays we often forget that it was the cosmopolitan Arab culture of Southern Spain, El Andalus, that was the great teacher of medieval Europe. As the Christians of Northern Spain reconquered the Muslim South, scholars from all countries of Europe flocked to Toledo and other centres to translate Arab documents on science and philosophy. The Arabs had surged out of the desert to conquer lands from India to Spain. In this way, they had come into contact with the learning of India, Persia, Babylon, Egypt and Greece, which they had absorbed into their culture. They also had significant trading contact with Tang China and knowledge of Chinese science and technology. Western science, mathematics, medicine, music, architecture and other fields of study were tremendously stimulated by contact with the advanced civilization of the Arabs. When I visited the graceful buildings and gardens of Andalusia, I tried to imagine El Andalus at the height of its brilliance.**

In modern times, Spain has experienced an economic miracle and construction boom that make it a different place from the country I visited in the 1960s, but the older Spain I first encountered had an unspoiled charm that I enjoyed very much. I visited Pamplona during the Fiesta de San Fermin on July 7. The whole town was engaged in a three day party of drinking and singing and conviviality. I could practice my Spanish in every little bar and restaurant. It was all very safe despite the drinking and revelry. I was mostly attracted to the partying and declined to risk my life running with the bulls. Besides, it required getting up very early in the morning.

Spain, especially in the South, is a country of strong impressions. The overpowering sun brings out the contrasts between sun and shade, between the dark tones of the trees and flowers, the brightness of the whitewashed houses and the stingy orange of the dry earth. As I was told in those days, "It is the sun which allows us to put up with Franco." Everywhere people were proud and friendly. My ability to communicate in Spanish enabled me to walk into every bodega and tapas bar, make friends, and explore the culture through the language.

Paris in the 1960s

While I enjoyed travel, my main purpose was to study. Paris in the early 1960s was a magical place. I lived in a small unheated and uncomfortable flat on the Rue du Faubourg St. Honoré in a building that was built in 1789. I was on the sixth floor and the toilet was on the third floor. I always knew if my neighbor below me on the fifth floor was home because I took a bath by pouring hot water into a small tub in my kitchen. It was just impossible not to spill some water, a few drops of which found their way down to my neighbor, who then banged on his ceiling with a broom-handle.

It is remarkable that a building with such poor standards of accommodation was located in a uniquely fashionable area of Paris. The world headquarters of some of the leading fashion and perfume companies of the world are on the Rue du Faubourg St. Honoré. Estée Lauder was in my building, for example. The Elysée Palace, home of the French President, was just down the street. The Place de la Concorde, *la plus belle place du monde,* was the next block over. And I lived in an unheated room that had not changed much since the French Revolution!

Within walking distance were the shops and eating places of the wealthy: Fauchon, the great caterer and food store on the Place de la Madeleine, the shops on the Grands Boulevards and Maxim's restaurant. This was the world of La Belle Époque, symbolizing to me the height of France's cultural influence preceding the tragic events of twentieth century Europe.

The Champs Elysées was just around the corner. I would often end my evenings strolling down this most beautiful boulevard. I would start in the Middle Ages at Notre Dame Cathedral, pass by the Renaissance at the Louvre, experience l'Ancien Régime as I walked through the Jardins des Tuileries designed by Louis XIV's gardener and then cross the Place de la Concorde where influences of the 18th and 19th century come together in balance and harmony. Continuing from there, it is hard not to fix one's attention on Napoleon Bonaparte's heroic Arc du Triomphe which overlooks the surrounding districts from the heights of the Place de L'Étoile. Despite the intent of Napoleon in building this monument to his victories, the lasting power of any civilization is not its force of arms, but its contribution to world civilization.

My bicycle took me everywhere I needed to go: to school, to my part time jobs, and out on the town in the Quartier Latin. Negotiating the traffic on the Place de la Concorde or Place de L'Étoile with my bicycle was a daily challenge. On the other hand, there was no better way to really experience the feeling of living in Paris. It was also the easiest and fastest way to get from point to point without worrying about parking.

I had several part time jobs. One involved taking lunch with French families while offering English conversation in return. As a poor student used to the simpler university restaurant fare, I always took advantage of these lunches to eat plenty of good food and have a few glasses of wine, finishing with a strong espresso coffee so I would not fall asleep. My second job had me running an English language lab at the French Agricultural Institute. Every Thursday, a plentiful lunch with a "bourgeois family" was followed by a bicycle ride halfway across Paris to the Agricultural Institute, on a full stomach. I arrived sweating profusely just in time to turn on the central controls for the language lab.

It was at the Agricultural Institute that a student walked out of the lab in disgust at his inability to understand English. I remember that the material we prepared for these students was full of technical agricultural terms but was otherwise of no interest to the young students. It is impossible to just learn vocabulary in the hope that one day it will be useful.

These farm boys at the Agricultural Institute could not speak English. What was the point of giving them obscure technical terms that they would probably never use? As is so often the case in language instruction, there was too much emphasis on grammar and vocabulary in order to prepare students for exams, rather than on how to communicate.

We can only learn to use a language from interesting and meaningful content. We should have allowed the students to choose subjects that were familiar and of interest to them. Some may have chosen farming, but many would probably have preferred to listen to recordings of genuine conversations in English between young people talking about music, or going to a party. The objective should have been to make English meaningful. Once these students were able to communicate, the technical vocabulary of agriculture could be learned quickly if necessary.

My First Real Job

Returning on my bicycle from a late night bowl of onion soup at Les Halles, the produce market featured in the movie *Irma La Douce*, I found a letter in my mailbox advising me that I had been accepted into the Canadian Foreign Trade Service. A friend of mine had persuaded me to write the Foreign Service exam at the Canadian Embassy some months earlier, and here I was now with a job!

This same friend and I had been planning to travel around the world on Honda motorcycles if Honda would sponsor us. The Foreign Service opportunity looked more promising.

As wonderful as my stay in France was, I often felt homesick for Canada. Going abroad allowed me to better understand and even to better appreciate my own home and original culture. Learning another language and culture does not take away from the enjoyment of your own background, it only intensifies it.

Yet I was destined to live abroad for many more years in Asia before finally settling down in Vancouver.

Discovering Asian Culture

Creating An Opportunity, Ottawa 1967

He who depends on himself will attain the greatest happiness.
– Yi Jing (Book of Changes), 2nd Millenium BC

I did not know when I entered the Canadian Diplomatic Service that I would end up being immersed in the cultures of both China and Japan. My language adventure would soon confront me with the challenge of learning languages that previously had seemed strange and distant to me. To achieve fluency in these languages required commitment, intensity and good learning techniques. But I could not have succeeded without a strong interest in the people and the culture, and the confidence that I would become a fluent speaker of these languages.

In 1967 in the Canadian capital city of Ottawa, I began my first full time job as an Assistant Trade Commissioner. Most of our group of young and eager Trade Commissioners-in-training had visions of serving their country in interesting foreign postings. However, fully one third of all Trade Commission posts are in the United States. Everyone wanted to avoid an assignment to Cleveland or Buffalo.

When the Trade Service announced that they were going to appoint an officer to Hong Kong to learn Chinese in preparation for the expected establishment of diplomatic relations with the People's Republic of China, I figured that this was my chance to avoid Buffalo.

I started taking Chinese lessons from an elderly Chinese man in Ottawa. While I did not learn much by merely taking lessons once a week, I let the Director of Personnel and other senior people know what I was doing. Given the opportunity, why would they not choose as a language student someone who was already committed to learning Chinese? Hong Kong was not my first choice as a posting; I was in fact more interested in getting to Rio de Janeiro or Rome or Madrid. But Hong Kong still sounded exotic.

I was very pleased when I was finally assigned to Hong Kong. I was obviously chosen because I had already made a commitment to learning the language. Commitment pays dividends in many ways. As to the choice of Hong Kong, in those days China was in the throes of the Cultural

Revolution and Taiwan was not politically acceptable for a future Canadian representative to The People's Republic of China. Instead, Hong Kong, with its Mandarin speaking émigré community, was the most suitable place to learn Chinese.

I remember that a good friend questioned whether I should accept the assignment. "What if you cannot learn Chinese?" he asked. But after my experience in mastering French, I had no doubt that I could master Chinese, too. The reason linguists can master several languages is largely because of their increased confidence. Language learning becomes demystified. Also, the more languages you learn, the more you develop the ability to cope with new ways of saying things. It is a bit like sports. A person who has developed fitness in one sport can more easily learn another sport.

My kindly Chinese teacher back in Ottawa had warned me to be wary of the charms of the attractive girls in Hong Kong but I did not heed his advice. I ended up finding my wife, Carmen, in Hong Kong and we are still happily married more than thirty years later, with two sons and five grandchildren. But I did not know that as I headed out to the exotic Far East for the first time.

Intensity, Hong Kong 1968

I had visions of Hong Kong as a romantic city with curved Chinese roofs and weeping willow trees. I was looking forward to immersing myself in this exotic environment. It was in June 1968 at the age of twenty-two that I headed out to Asia for the first time. I took holidays on my way to Hong Kong and I was able to experience parts of the world that I had previously visited only in my imagination: in Italy, the magnificence of Rome and its disorderly traffic; in Israel, the timelessness of a starlit summer night over the ancient city of Jerusalem and the tension of a country after a recent war; in Iran, the exoticism of the Teheran bazaar and its reckless taxis bedecked with Christmas lights in June; in India, the splendour of the Taj Mahal and the turmoil of life in New Delhi; and in Thailand, the bright colours of Bangkok and the elegance of its people and culture. My excitement about my new assignment in Hong Kong was building throughout my trip.

Finally I touched down in Hong Kong, where I was met by the official car of the Canadian High Commission. As we drove through congested Kowloon with its forest of drab, gray, high-rise apartment buildings, I was suddenly brought back to reality. Hong Kong was no Shangri-la. However, as our car got onto the vehicular ferry to cross over from Kowloon to Hong Kong Island, I was suddenly treated to a waterborne kaleidoscope of ocean freighters, barges, war ships, Chinese junks and pleasure crafts against a backdrop of modern skyscrapers and stately colonial buildings, all overlooked by Victoria Peak on the Hong Kong side.

Living in the Crown Colony of Hong Kong, as it was called in those days, I always felt a little hemmed in. Before you could go anywhere you had to fly out or take a boat. China was essentially closed, and this could be depressing. However, the least expensive way to cheer myself up was to pay ten or fifteen Hong Kong cents to cross the harbour on the Star Ferry. I never got tired of studying the skyline and the traffic on the water during this fifteen minute crossing.

For the first months I lived on the Hong Kong side near Stanley and Repulse Bay. I had an unobstructed view of a romantic little bay where I could satisfy my desire for the exotic by studying the Chinese transport junks plying up and down the sparkling turquoise waters of the South China Sea. This relatively sparsely populated part of the Crown Colony had beaches, leafy semi-tropical vegetation and a large European population. It was like a resort. I was expected to live there and attend the Hong Kong University where all previous diplomatic language students had studied. But after a few months I chose to live and study on the more densely populated Kowloon side, and I enrolled at the Chinese University of Hong Kong. Just as I had wanted to immerse myself in French culture in order to learn French, I took the same attitude towards my Chinese learning.

Soon after arriving in Hong Kong I met my future wife, Carmen, at a party attended by members of the Canadian community. Carmen was the fluently bilingual secretary to the General Manager of Canadian Pacific Airlines. With a Chinese father and Costa Rican mother, Carmen had a unique vivacity and zest for life that was increasingly irresistible to me (and I did not try too hard to resist). She became my guide to Hong Kong in those days. I had a small Vespa scooter and whenever I was not studying Chinese, we were usually visiting some restaurant or remote beach or interesting market. The only disadvantage to this relationship was that Carmen was not a Mandarin speaker. She was fluent in English, as well as Cantonese, so we spoke English all the time. Ah well, you cannot have everything!

Carmen's grandfather, from Yan Ping in Guangdong province, had traveled to Costa Rica and opened a store there in the late 1890's. He was one of the early Chinese immigrants who ventured into Latin America to seek their fortune. He eventually returned to Macao where he built a peanut oil factory. But this factory was turned over to his youngest son and favourite, who squandered this asset while the three older sons, including Yan Tong, Carmen's father, were sent to Costa Rica to earn money for the family.

When Yan Tong returned to Macao in the late 1930's he brought back his young Costa Rican bride Marta and two young daughters, Carmen's older sisters. Marta was an awkward figure as the only "guai po" (foreign woman) in an extended Chinese family. Marta had to learn fast. She had to figure out how to be a wife and a mother in a strange culture. She was to be busy raising eleven children, including three that were not her own.

The Chinese language was at first a frustrating obstacle for her. She was often homesick for Costa Rica. With her knowledge of Spanish she managed to make a few friends amongst the Portuguese in Macao, with whom she could communicate more comfortably. In time she learned Cantonese, which is the language she spoke with her children and other family members. Now at the age of 88, retired in Toronto, she is happiest going for meals in Chinatown and chatting with the waiters in Cantonese. Language can either be a barrier or a lifelong source of pleasure and satisfaction.

Hong Kong, like Macao, is Cantonese speaking, and therefore does not offer immersion in Mandarin. However, it is Chinese and did offer an intense exposure to Chinese culture. I was taken out of my comfortable Western cocoon and exposed daily to the sounds and smells of the busy streets and markets, the shops selling Chinese medicine and other exotic products, the energy of so many people bustling in street-side workshops or peddling products they often carried balanced on a pole. Near my school or in the crowded Tsimshatsui district of Kowloon, I could eat inexpensive noodles or curry rice lunches with workers or enjoy sumptuous Cantonese meals in luxury restaurants. There were numerous restaurants representing the cuisine of many different parts of China: Beijing, Shandong, Sichuan, Chao Zhou and more, all squeezed into narrow, crowded streets. This was my daily living environment as I studied Chinese. Indirectly I was being conditioned to accept the language.

To me, food and language are the most enjoyable and accessible features of a culture, and in my mind they are closely connected. I still remember my lunch-time conversations in Mandarin with my teachers, over Hui

Guo Rou (braised garlic pork), Man Tou (steamed bread) and eel soup. These informal gatherings were my most pleasant and relaxed learning experiences. The teachers would talk of their childhood in China or other interesting subjects. At a Chinese meal, everyone helps themselves from common serving dishes with their chopsticks. I have always had a good appetite, and as the only Canadian at the table I was quickly nicknamed "jia na da" ("Canada" in Mandarin) with the emphasis on "na da," meaning "to reach and take a big piece."

I made the right decision in choosing the Chinese University of Hong Kong. The Chinese Language School was run by one of the most effective language teachers I have met, Mr. Liu Ming. He welcomed people to the Chinese language and made foreigners feel that they could learn Mandarin. He insisted on hard work from the learner, because he himself was an energetic and hard-working man. He inspired me to commit to my new language challenge and was always flexible in accommodating my requests. The staff of the language school were very friendly and encouraging.

At first I was dependent on my one-on-one sessions with the teachers. However, soon I began to find the classes were a strain. I was obliged to go to class for three hours every morning. Sometimes I was tired and hardly able to pay attention. The effectiveness of the teachers varied. Some teachers were intent on giving me explanations in English, which I found particularly irksome. The fashion in those days was to emphasize drills, which were often tiring and annoying. The best sessions were those when the teacher would just talk about some interesting subject. I did most of my learning at these more informal conversational sessions as well as when studying intensely at home.

It was the energy of the Director, Liu Ming, who watched over us and challenged us that really inspired me to work hard. The texts we used were from the Yale-in-China program. The first text was called *Chinese Dialogues* and was set in the China of the pre-Liberation period. The dialogues described a certain Mr. Smith living, working and traveling around in China from Shanghai to Nanking and Beiping (as it was called in the Kuomintang days). This context was divorced from the reality of late 1960s China, which was caught up in the Cultural Revolution. I remember very little of the content of this textbook, but I realize that an artificial text like this is probably necessary at the beginning stage of learning a language.

The first period of language learning is both difficult and satisfying. It is difficult because the language seems so strange, yet it is satisfying because in a short period of time you learn to say a few things in a new language. In these beginning stages the language you are learning is not natural, but content especially prepared for the learner, covering such scenarios as the post office, the train station, a restaurant, meeting a family and so on. Beginner language courses are available in bookstores. In my experience it does not matter which system you use at first as long as you find it to your taste. You need to spend most of your time listening and reading, without trying to master the details of grammar. These beginner programs will get you past the initial stage and provide you with some of the basic vocabulary and structure.

Once you reach the intermediate stage you face the longest and most demanding part of your task. You now want to achieve a breakthrough to fluency. You need to move from being able to say a few things in a limited social setting to being able to use the language as a practical means of communication in a variety of situations that you do not control. To do this requires a commitment to reading and listening to a great deal of language content. If the content is interesting you will enjoy the learning process and do well. Artificial dialogues and uninteresting "learner" content soon outlive their usefulness. Fortunately I was able to move to meaningful content quite soon in my study of Chinese.

Reading and Vocabulary Growth

Intermediate readers can be useful as long as you are interested in the content. Unfortunately, most learners are not given much choice. In my study of Chinese I was lucky. The next reader we had in our program was a book I still recommend. It is called *Twenty Lectures in Chinese Culture*. Developed at Yale in 1963 as an early reader, this book covers Chinese history and culture, in simple straightforward language. I still occasionally read the book to refresh my Chinese. Although the book is written for learners in simple language, the subject is real: Chinese culture and history.

After about four months, I read only authentic Chinese content, mostly using readers which had specially prepared vocabulary lists. The subjects varied from history to politics to literature. Suddenly, a fascinating world opened up to me in the original language. The wonderful Yale-in-China series, "Readings in Contemporary Chinese Literature", offered a wide range of essays, plays, political commentary, and short stories by leading writers, thinkers and political figures of early 20ᵗʰ century China.

Lu Xun is one of the authors whose works are most widely available to foreign learners of Chinese. Lu Xun was one of the most respected writers of this period. He abandoned his medical studies to devote himself to writing in order to expose the weaknesses he saw in traditional Chinese society. His essays and short stories were harsh clinical diagnoses of illnesses in society that he wanted to cure. Frequent themes were the superstition and passivity of the common people, and the "Quixotic" pride of certain members of the intellectual classes. With his negative portrait of the old society, Lu Xun was a favourite in post-"Liberation" China. As Mao Tse Tung was fond to say, "you have to know the bitterness of the past to understand the sweetness of the present".

One of my favourite stories by Lu Xun was "Kong Yi Ji", about a pathetic village vagrant at the turn of the 20ᵗʰ century, who would come to drink at a small wine house frequented by workers. He was dirty and unkempt but wore the long gown of the intellectual class rather than the short jackets worn by the working class. He made a paltry living from his ability at calligraphy, but drank too much and often stole books and writing utensils from people. He would speak using literary terms, which only earned him scorn and laughter from the others at the wine house. In the end he was caught stealing and beaten so badly that he could only crawl back to the wine house for a last drink. After that he was not seen again. Lu perhaps meant this story as a critique of the intellectual class of the old China, or the callous indifference of some people to the suffering of others. What I appreciated in the story was the description of the wine house, the people, the wine, the huixiangdou or spicy beans that would be eaten with the wine, and the realistic portrayal of the characters. I felt that I would like to visit that village and sit down and have a cup of warm rice wine and chat with the locals. That was the effect of most of my reading of Chinese stories. It just made me want to visit China and experience life there.

The first novel I attempted to read without the help of a word list was Lao She's novel, Rickshaw Boy, a human and sympathetic description of life in Beijing, without the bitterness that I found in the writings of Lu Xun and others. It took a long time to finish the book but I felt very satisfied when I completed it. There were many words that I did not know. Mostly I avoided looking them up in a dictionary so that I could enjoy the book.

There comes a point in language learning when you have to read a full length book in the new language. In most language learning programs the learner is conditioned to deal only with short excerpts. Completing a full length book is like climbing a mountain. Nowadays, with electronic texts, it has become much easier to struggle through authentic material, look up the meaning using dictionary software, and save words and phrases for systematic learning. Since there are still many characters I do not know, I look forward to doing more reading in Chinese once The Linguist system is available for that language.

My commitment to learning Chinese was quite fanatical, and I guess that is what enabled me learn Chinese in such a short period of time. I lived much like a hermit devoting myself to the intensive study of Chinese. I spent more time with my books and tapes than with people. For the first stage in learning a new language it is more efficient to spend time on an intensive self-directed program of concentrated language input until you are ready to meaningfully converse with native speakers. Conversations with native speakers are a stimulus to more effort, but can be frustrating when you have only a limited ability to communicate. I had my tape recorder on from the time I woke up, either in the background or at intensive sessions where I concentrated on pronunciation. I worked hard to learn Chinese characters, writing them down and reviewing them daily. I read as much as I could, and reread the same material frequently to improve my ability at reading Chinese writing. I studied the vocabulary lists that went with these texts. It always seemed as if I could never remember new words, but eventually they stuck with me.

Since Hong Kong is not a Mandarin speaking city, I could not just go out and talk to shopkeepers or others in Mandarin. While there were some Mandarin radio and television programs, I found I could only understand some of the language and then it was gone. On the other hand, I found that using a tape recorder to listen over and over again to material that I already understood was very beneficial to my learning. The problem was getting hold of enough interesting audio content at my level of comprehension.

When I lived in Hong Kong, tape recorders were not portable. Those were still the days of the open reel tape recorders that were large, heavy and awkward. I had to sit at home and listen. Today, modern technology makes it possible to easily find material of interest to download or record so you can take your listening everywhere.

Since Chinese essentially has no phonetic script, I had to learn three to four thousand characters, each requiring as many as fifteen or more strokes. Needless to say, vocabulary acquisition is more difficult than in English. I realized that the dictionary had to be the last resort of the language learner. Looking words up in a conventional dictionary is one of the least efficient and most wasteful activities of language learning. Very often you forget the meaning of the word as soon as you close the dictionary. Using a Chinese Dictionary is even more difficult than looking up a word in a language based on an alphabet.

One of the frustrations we all face in language learning is the speed with which we forget newly learned words. It seems as if everything has to be learned and relearned so many times. In Chinese, this is an even greater problem because of the difficulty of learning the characters. I had to find a way to increase my speed of learning characters.

I developed techniques of working with new vocabulary items that enabled me to reinforce learning and vocabulary retention. One system was based on the way Chinese children learn characters. I bought exercise books that were divided into squares for writing characters. I would start writing a character six or seven times down the first column and then write the sound or English meaning on the third column. Then I would start a second character and do the same. Soon I ran into the first character I had learned and had to write it again. In other words, I reminded myself regularly of words that I had just learned before I had a chance to forget them. At first I could only learn ten new characters a day but after a while I was up to thirty per day, with roughly a fifty percent retention rate. The retention rate was higher if the words were connected to content that I was reading or listening to. This principle of systematically relearning new words until they start to stick has been carried over to all my language learning.

It was important for me to write Chinese, even though my calligraphy was poor. When I wrote Chinese I had the time to compose my sentences and choose my words carefully. Writing helped me reinforce my vocabulary. It also was an opportunity to practice sentence structure.

In modern Chinese the written language is similar to the spoken language, and my writing certainly was. Chinese classics, on the other hand, are written in an elegant short hand quite different from the spoken language. Modern Chinese writers often include some of this more refined language in their prose. I did not bother with that. My Chinese writing was simple and direct, quite sufficient to translate newspaper editorials or whatever I was given as a study assignment. Making my writing a sort of extension of my spoken language helped me improve my ability to express myself in Chinese. Language learners should write often, and they should minimize any differences between their written and spoken language.

Another principle of learning new vocabulary that has stuck with me is the importance of context. It is easier to remember the meanings of Chinese characters in compound words consisting of two or more characters than individually. I still have difficulty recognizing certain characters on their own but easily can identify the meanings of characters in compound words. This principle of learning words in the context of phrases and larger content is useful in any language, and became a fundamental feature of the learning system we developed.

The Importance of Phrases

The principles of Chinese grammar are different from English. I deliberately ignored explanations of the theory of Chinese grammar because these theoretical explanations made no sense to me. Instead, I just accepted the various structural patterns of sentences in Chinese as normal. I knew that with enough exposure they would start to seem natural to me. I found it easier to learn the structure of a new language from frequent exposure to phrase patterns rather than trying to understand abstract grammatical explanations of that structure. I realized in studying Chinese, a language so different from my own, that the fundamental component I had to learn was not the word, but the phrase. Language skill consists of spontaneously being able to use prefabricated phrases and phrase patterns that are natural to the native speaker and need to become natural to the learner.

Phrases are the best models of correct practice in a language. Certain words naturally belong together in a way that the learner cannot anticipate but can only try to get used to. When words are combined in the natural phrases of the language they achieve force and clarity. It is not grammar and words that need to be learned, so much as phrases. New vocabulary is more easily learned together with the phrases where it is found, and even pronunciation should be learned in the form of phrases. Phrases, however, cannot be easily learned from lists. Rather it is when the same phrases are frequently encountered in audio and written contexts and then systematically studied and used that you are able to retain them.

Pronunciation

We are all capable of correctly pronouncing the sounds of any foreign language. All humans have the same physiological ability to make sounds, regardless of ethnic origin. However, mastering the pronunciation of a new language does require dedication and hard work. Chinese, at first, represented quite a challenge.

When I wanted to master pronunciation I would spend hours every day listening to the same content over and over. I worked especially hard on mastering Chinese sounds with the appropriate tone. I tried to imitate while listening. I taped my own voice and compared it to the native speaker. I practiced reading in a loud voice. Eventually my ability to hear the differences between my pronunciation and that of the native speaker improved. I would force my mouth to conform to the needs of Chinese pronunciation. I would also work on the rhythm of the new language, always exaggerating and even accompanying my pronunciation with the appropriate facial expressions and gestures. Eventually I was able to achieve a near native quality of pronunciation.

Once I was able to pronounce individual words and phrases satisfactorily, I would find it easier to understand content not designed for the learner; in other words, authentic material. I would record radio broadcasts to listen to over and over. Much later when I had reached a certain level of fluency, I particularly enjoyed listening to the famous Beijing Xiang Sheng comic dialogue performer Hou Bao Lin, with his colourful Beijing rhythm of speech. In recent years, to maintain my Mandarin, I sometimes listen to CDs of famous Chinese storytellers, like Yuan Kuo Cheng, narrating classic novels such as *The Romance of the Three Kingdoms*. The storytelling art in China is highly developed and when I listen to one of these CDs I thoroughly enjoy being transported back to a bygone era.

After about nine months of study I wrote and passed the British Government Foreign Service examination in Mandarin. We were tested on translations from Chinese to English and from English to Chinese. There was also an oral exam. I even had to write a diplomatic note in Chinese, a skill that I have never had occasion to use. With that, my study of Chinese was considered complete, although I have never stopped learning since then.

I started working at the Canadian High Commission, as a Second Secretary, dealing with Canada's trade with the People's Republic of China. My work consisted of responding to enquiries from Canadian businessmen, finding out information about the market and meeting with officials of Chinese trading corporations in Hong Kong. I also attended the twice annual Canton International Trade Fair. I had ample opportunity to speak and read Chinese.

Hong Kong was a centre of "China Watching" as people tried to glean from newspapers, radio and returning travelers what was really happening in China during the period of turbulence known as the Great Proletarian Cultural Revolution. I had to learn about China's agricultural economy since China was a major export market for Canadian wheat. A Chinese booked called Economic Geography of China gave a clear description of the production, distribution and consumption of grain in China. I was also able to research news reports related to agriculture. From all of this I prepared reports for our government, which, in retrospect, were probably not very useful to anyone. But I did enjoy putting my Chinese language skills to use.

I got to know some Mandarin speakers who had recently left China or who seemed well informed about happenings there. They were a colourful group. As I remember it now, one member of this group was a Mr. Lung, a member of a national minority from Southwest China and the son of a famous political figure in the old China. His beautiful wife was of Manchurian origin and, according to some, related to the ruling family of China under the Qing dynasty. I liked Mr. Lung who was a charming gentleman. His brother, a well known party-going playboy known as Prince Lung, was married to a famous movie star who is reputed to have committed suicide because of her husband's infidelity. By and large this group was not supportive of the Cultural Revolution.

There were others who were "leftists", including Percy Chan of mixed Caribbean-Chinese origin, the son of China's first Foreign Minister under the Nationalists. These "leftists" would explain how the Cultural Revolution was going to create a wonderful new society in China that would be a model to the world. There was no shortage of similar apologists for the New China amongst Western leftist intellectuals. Many intellectuals need to feel that they are in possession of some insight or moral truth that is not available to the average person. That is why they are easily taken in by the latest ideological fashion. I wonder what Zhuangzi would have thought of the convoluted ideological and political struggles taking place in China at that time.

The world of the thirties in China was far removed from the reality of China in the late 1960s. Pre-Liberation China was full of tragedy, poverty, and uncertainty. China was torn apart by internal rivalries between different political forces and selfish local warlords, while fighting off foreign invasion. These were cruel and hard times. Yet to me, China was fascinating and even romantic. With enough distance in time or space, periods of warfare and struggle can seem heroic. *The Romance of the Three Kingdoms*, the epic Chinese novel, or the glorification of the knights of Medieval Europe, are but two examples of how legend and literature romanticize periods of terrible human suffering. Chinese society was looking for its place in a world where foreign influence had all of a sudden collided with a complex, brilliant and previously self-contained Chinese civilization in decline.

The Chinese intellectual class that had been one of the main supports of traditional China was now searching for its new role. Some Chinese intellectuals were defenders of Chinese orthodoxy, some were champions of the new revolutionary thought of Marxism, and yet others, like Dr. Hu Shih, were extremely sophisticated explainers of Western philosophy and its relevance to the new China, and even of its relationship with Chinese philosophy.

The historic evolution of China was different from that of Western Asia and the Mediterranean. The power of the Chinese central state proved more durable than the power of Egypt, Mesopotamia, Greece or Rome. As Chinese culture and people spread and mixed with local ethnic groups in South China, no permanent separate states sprang up as was the case in Europe with the interaction of Romans and other peoples. In the North of China, constant invasions and settlement by Turkic, Mongolian, Tibetan and Tungusic peoples were a dominant feature for 2,000 years. Yet, throughout this period, the prestige and power of Chinese culture was not permanently challenged. This is in part because of the flexibility of the Chinese writing system, which could be used to represent meaning even if words were pronounced differently. China was able to maintain its unity while absorbing diverse cultural and ethnic elements in different regions of the country.

It is impossible to look at the refined scenes from Chinese paintings of the Tang or Song periods without admiring the high standard of living and sophistication of Chinese society of the time, compared to the lower level of culture at the same period in Europe. It is interesting to speculate what this technically and culturally sophisticated Chinese society would have created under different historical circumstances. But then, change is the only constant of the human condition.

> We in the Western world do not learn enough in school about the involvement of Chinese civilization with other parts of the world. The beneficiaries of Chinese culture were not only neighboring East Asian countries, who borrowed heavily from Chinese culture, but also Western Europe. The introduction of Chinese technology to Europe in the Early Middle Ages was instrumental in stimulating progress in technology and navigation.

Crossing Into China, Canton 1969

In 1969 I was finally able to see the China of my imagination, and to use Mandarin in an environment where it was the national language. I crossed into China from Hong Kong at the Lowu bridge near a small village called Shen Zhen. From the waiting room of the train station I could just make out the rows of low traditional peasant houses behind the posters with slogans exhorting the people to greater revolutionary efforts. Today, this quiet village has become one of the largest cities in China, a vast urban sprawl of modern skyscrapers and thriving capitalism, and a leader in technology, fashion and more.

As a foreigner, I was automatically seated in the soft seat section on the train to Canton (today's Guangzhou). This entitled me to a cup of flower tea, which was regularly refreshed with more hot water by an attendant as the train rode through Southern Guangdong Province with its hills of red earth and green rice fields. I strained to listen to the constant political messages being broadcast on the train's public address system.

In Canton I stayed at the Dong Fang Hotel, a Soviet style hotel which accommodated the European and North American businessmen. The Japanese and Overseas Chinese stayed elsewhere, according to the arrangements of the Chinese authorities.

China was caught up in the turmoil of the Cultural Revolution. Early every morning the guests of the Dong Fang Hotel were wakened to the stirring strains of Chinese revolutionary and patriotic music. The walls of the city were covered in slogans. The air of this southern city was heavy with warm humidity and tension. Military personnel were in evidence everywhere.

To a foreigner visiting for a short period, Canton seemed pleasant. There was very little traffic. The semi-tropical vegetation of Canton's many parks was lush and green. The pace of life appeared leisurely, especially when compared to the hustle of Hong Kong. In addition, the legendary cuisine of Canton did not disappoint. There was a selection of excellent restaurants at reasonable prices

The restaurants in Hong Kong were busy and noisy places. Canton was different. At the Northern Garden or Southern Garden, or other famous restaurants, we dined elegantly, in peaceful and classical Chinese surroundings, for a fraction of the cost of Hong Kong. The waiters were older and served us with refinement and a high degree of professional pride. The dishes were not only tasty, but a feast for the eyes, sometimes arranged to look like multi-coloured peacocks or flowers. Cantonese food, subtle and light, with an emphasis on slightly braised fresh vegetables and seafood, is well suited to the semi-tropical climate of the South.

We would usually gather a group of eight to ten people and then rent a few taxis to go to one of these restaurants. We accompanied our meal with beer and maotai, a powerful vodka-like liquor. Drinking maotai is more of an endurance contest than a treat for the taste buds, but it was an obligatory part of our dinner ritual. We would toast each other in the fashion of the Chinese, and even play Chinese drinking games. In one such game we would put the head of a chicken on a plate and place a bowl over it. The plate was then spun around several times and the bowl removed. Whoever was sitting where the chicken head was pointing, had to down a glass of maotai. On one occasion, while enjoying our food and drink we could hear gunfire in the distance as rival gangs of Red guards fought each other.

In all of these restaurants we ate in special areas reserved for foreigners. In a similar fashion there were Friendship Stores reserved for foreigners. At one time there was even a special currency for use only by foreigners. The Chinese authorities tried to segregate foreigners from the average Chinese citizen. Nevertheless, I was occasionally able to engage people in conversation on the street, using my Mandarin. Most people were reluctant to talk to a foreigner but some would open up. Once on a street in Canton there was a man, probably in his thirties, who looked at me and then pointed to an old bus and said, "Do you see that bus? It is old and run down, just like China. Do you know what is worse? We will never get a new bus and things will never improve here." I hope he is still alive today to see the changes that have taken place in China.

Perhaps the austerity of the Cultural Revolution seemed particularly unfriendly to the many foreign visitors who could not understand Chinese.

I remember once in Canton when a German businessman, fed up with political slogans at his business meetings and blaring from loudspeakers, and having had far too much beer to drink at the bar of the Dung Fang hotel, threw his beer glass at a picture of Chairman Mao! Perhaps an anti-establishment free thinker like Zhuangzi would have appreciated the spirit of this gesture, but the staff of the hotel were not amused. This German businessman was immediately seized, his bags packed and he was literally thrown out of China. He was lucky not to have met a worse fate.

Even in poor times, food is important to Chinese people. In China, people do not walk down the street eating a sandwich as North Americans sometimes do. People take the time to eat. As I walked the streets of Canton, I would see shop workers and others gather around common dishes of tasty vegetables and a few pieces of meat, as well as rice, for their noon meal. Even when we visited a rather poor peoples' commune near Canton during the Cultural Revolution, the people were dressed in patched clothing, but the country cooking was delicious and healthy.

Still, it was impossible not to notice the mood of tension and discouragement among many of the people. Being a foreign diplomat, I was assigned a guide from the China Travel Service whose duty it was to keep an eye on me. We spoke in Chinese and exchanged views on many subjects. One day I asked him how he put up with the constant barrage of slogans. My guide, a product of Mao's China and obviously security-cleared to guide foreign diplomats replied, "It is like Dr. Goebbels said in the Second World War. If you tell a lie a thousand times, it becomes the truth!" So much for stereotypes! Far from accepting all the propaganda, this person was well read and had an opinion of his own. I was amazed!

China Travel Service was supposed to be a travel company, but under the Cultural Revolution, serving the customer was not a major priority. If a foreign businessman asked what there was to see in Canton, the answer was often a lazy and uninterested, "What do you want to see?"

Every so often China Travel would tell us that they had good news. "You are going to see Revolutionary Opera," and off we would go. These performances were the latest revisions of a small number of shows that were constantly being edited and approved for ideological content by Jiang Qing (Chairman Mao's wife), leader of the Gang of Four who ran China in those days. These "revolutionary operas" were a mixture of modern and old, of Chinese and Western, and were a little tiring to sit through, especially the second and third time. It was much later that I had an opportunity to see real Peking Opera. The costumes and sound effects were spectacular, and the music haunting in its evocation of a different time and culture.

While China Travel was not a customer oriented travel agency during the Cultural Revolution, the language ability of their guides was always impressive. For most of my visits to China during the late sixties and early seventies, as a foreign diplomat, I was obliged to have an interpreter-guide. There were speakers of many different languages. Once, however, visiting a rural area in Guangdong province, my wife had to translate since the China Travel guide could not speak Cantonese. On another occasion, visiting Shanghai on holiday from Japan, my wife and I had a Japanese speaking guide since all English speaking guides were busy. Somehow or other we always managed to communicate.

The standard of the translators I met in China was always high. Yet, it is inevitable that translators will make mistakes. I am no exception when I have to interpret. It is not possible to remember every word and to always know the emphasis that the speaker intended. Furthermore there are many people who speak their own language poorly which makes the interpreter's job even more difficult. Interpreters are proud professionals and obviously do not like to be corrected. Often at business meetings there were mistranslations by our Chinese interpreter. I would just make a note of it for later. If the point was important, I would usually say something like, "I would like to add another point," rather than saying that something was mistranslated.

It is uncomfortable to be dependent on interpreters and translators. I think there has been a tendency to consider foreign language fluency as a skill for specialists and not something we all should have. Most business discussions in China used to be facilitated by a translator, and probably still are. Yet knowledge of Chinese is most helpful in creating contacts and deeper understanding. Hopefully, more foreigners will learn Chinese as the country opens up to more exchange with the rest of the world. Certainly, more Chinese people are fluent in English today than ever before. Even with the use of interpreters, it is very useful to understand one's counterpart's language. In an era of intense exchanges by phone and email, direct communication without translators is already becoming a reality. This trend will only increase.

Throughout 1969 and 1970 I was a regular visitor to the Canton International Trade Fair in my capacity as a Trade Commissioner. I was there to help Canadian businessmen in their discussions with the representatives of Chinese trading corporations. During the Cultural Revolution, the discussion was about politics as much as it was about business, much to the frustration of visiting Canadians. I tried to understand what was really going on in China but it was rather difficult. One good source of information was the colourful caricatures of leading political figures that would suddenly appear on the walls of the city. These posters were outstanding examples of the caricaturist's art.

Around that time, Canada was involved in negotiations with China to establish diplomatic relations. I discovered that Canada did not have its own interpreter present and relied on the Chinese side to do the interpreting. Even though I was a lowly language student, I immediately wrote a letter to the director of Canada's Foreign Service. I protested that not to use our own interpreter was demeaning to Canada's image and discouraging to those of us who were studying Chinese for the government. I recommended that my colleague Martin Collacott, who had been studying for a year longer than me, should be assigned to the negotiations. Martin was soon on his way to Stockholm, where the negotiations were taking place.

In 1970, Canada established diplomatic relations with the People's Republic of China. In October of that year, I accompanied the first Canadian delegation to Beijing for a short ten-day visit to help locate an Embassy building for Canada and make other administrative arrangements. The old city with its grey walls and hidden courtyards felt like one big forbidden city. The Imperial Palace (also known officially as The Forbidden City), built in the Ming Dynasty, is majestic in its scale. It is a suitable setting for the Imperial Palace of the most populous country with the longest continuous history in the world.

In the *Hutungs* or lanes which surrounded it, I was reminded of Lao She's famous novel, *Rickshaw Boy*. These narrow lanes are a maze of grey walls which hide courtyards where people live their lives away from the view of passers-by. I pictured to myself the people behind these walls quietly carrying on the traditions of Chinese culture: painting, calligraphy, Peking Opera, or poetry, while outside in the name of the Cultural Revolution the authorities were trying to discredit this very legacy for reasons of their own.

Beijing, except for its famous monuments, is not beautiful. To me it conjures up the frontier with Inner Asia. Beijing was never the centre of gravity of the Chinese state. For much of China's history it was a place of contact with the people of the steppe. A highlight of our visit to Beijing that year was an outing to the Great Wall, where for thousands of years the settled civilization of China tried to keep out the warlike nomadic peoples who envied China's riches. The influences of Inner Asia are noticeable in the heavier physical features of the people of Beijing and the climate. It was October when we were there and the weather was already getting colder. People wore thick layers of cotton clothing. Great mountains of cabbage were being dumped on street corners for people to buy and pickle for the winter.

As Imperial Capital for most of the last 800 years, Beijing has become a centre of learning and preservation of Chinese tradition. Influences from all over China mix in the capital. When we visited in 1970 we ate caviar every morning for breakfast, which had come from the Ussuri River. We dined on Peking duck and had dinner in a Mongolian Restaurant that dated from the 1400s. Much of the political leadership seemed to be from Central China. In those days, there were no modern buildings and the city looked much as it had for centuries. There was little traffic, other than the bicycles fighting a stiff autumn wind blowing in from the Central Asian steppes. Beijing is austere; quite different form the rich green rice fields, abundant water resources and elegant towns of the Yangtze delta, such as Suzhou and Hangzhou near Shanghai, which I visited in 1975.

While living in Japan during the 1970s I would try to find business or personal reasons to visit China. Going to Shanghai from Tokyo with my family in the summer of 1974 was like traveling back thirty years in time. The Shanghai waterfront had magnificent buildings dating from the 1930s and earlier, but little had been built since. Even in Shanghai foreigners were a rarity. With Carmen and our two small children we walked down Nanjing Street and were soon surrounded by people staring at us. People were just curious and in no way threatening, but our children started to cry. As we moved on the crowds dispersed. I have never felt uncomfortable in China because I speak the language. On the other hand, when I visit countries where I do not speak the language, like Finland, Hungary, or Russia, I feel less at ease.

Today, Shanghai is a modern city and the mood has completely changed. This change in mood has happened gradually. On a visit in the late 1970's an excellent small jazz band, consisting of musicians in their late fifties, were entertaining guests at the Peace Hotel in Shanghai. They played "decadent" western music. They even wore neckties! Not only was the music delightful, but seeing the obvious enjoyment of the band members who were once again allowed to perform greatly added to the festive atmosphere that they created.

One day, on a visit to Beijing in 1981, there was a notice at my hotel, the Friendship Hotel, that there was a dance planned for that evening. Of course I bought a ticket. I went there not knowing what to expect, sat at a table, ordered a beer and waited. Then suddenly a dozen or so lovely young ladies from the neighbouring dance academy came in. I had a delightful evening dancing with these ladies while thinking to myself that this scene was almost like a dream compared to the China that I had known ten or so years earlier. As China opened up, I was able to have more conversations with average people, who today are generally quite willing to strike up conversations with Chinese speaking foreigners. The taxi drivers of Beijing are especially friendly and talkative.

In 1981, while President of MacMillan-Bloedel Asia, based in Tokyo, I visited North East China with Charles Tai of our Hong Kong office, to learn about China's forest industry. In Harbin we were hosted one evening by officials of the local forest industry. We reciprocated the following evening. To outdo our hosts of the night before, we made sure that our banquet consisted of famous local delicacies such as deer's nose and bear's paw, as well as maotai. I asked a Chinese guest at dinner what was so special about maotai. He explained that it had "hui xiang" or returning fragrance. I drank copious amounts of maotai that evening, matching toasts with our Chinese counterparts. I still remember seeing my hotel room ceiling swimming overhead before falling into a deep sleep. The next morning as I woke up, I experienced maotai's "hui xiang."

As usual, my knowledge of Chinese is what made these trips so enjoyable. One night I traveled alone by night train across the vast plains of Heilongjiang province. There were no individual compartments in the sleeping car. It was just one big moving bedroom with 30 or 40 strangers. Had I not spoken Chinese I might have felt uncomfortable. I struck up a conversation with the person who had the bunk below me. He described his life in a small one-story brick house. His family fermented cabbage in a hole in the ground inside their home in order to have some vegetables to eat during the winter. With the temperature at 30 below, he and his wife would get up at 5.30 in the morning to start a fire to heat the house and cook their rice. The harshness of his life contrasted with the comfort of mine, but he did not seem unhappy. In many ways his life was not so different from the lives of Canadians who settled our prairie region as recently as the first half of the twentieth century. Through our common language, Chinese, we were able to develop a feeling of comradeship as we traveled through the night.

China today is moving rapidly to create a new modern society. Returning to China in 2001, after a long absence, I found the rate of new construction and the transformation of China simply unbelievable. After all my efforts at learning Chinese, thanks to the changes taking place in China today, I will finally have opportunities to use Mandarin regularly and develop business and personal relationships with ordinary Chinese people. This is very satisfying, since the goal of language study is communication with people.

Now that China has turned its back on the Cultural Revolution there is a renewal in both new and traditional arts, showing the strength and depth of cultural traditions and talents in China. I believe the world can look forward to an explosion of creativity from China, as long as the economy can continue to grow and provide more and more opportunities for individual expression. There is an atmosphere of impatience in today's China. After so many false starts in the previous century, people are probably afraid to really believe in their own success. Presumably this confidence will come with time.

Working and Learning in Japan

Sumeba miyako.
(free translation) Home is where you make it.
– *Japanese saying*

Having studied Chinese, I was expected to be assigned to Beijing as Assistant Trade Commissioner back in 1970. Instead, I refused to go. The reason was a major personality conflict with my immediate boss, the person designated to be Senior Trade Commissioner in Beijing. I felt it would be unpleasant to work in a post like Beijing where we would be quite isolated from the general population, if I could not get along with my superior. I promised the Trade Commissioner Service that I would learn Japanese on my own if reassigned to Tokyo. In this way the government would recoup some value from their investment in my language training. My superiors agreed.

I consider myself lucky to have lived in Montreal, Paris, Hong Kong, Tokyo, and now Vancouver. All of these cities have personality. Montreal manages to inspire its citizens with a certain Latin élan in a harsh climate that can only be compared to Moscow amongst major world cities. Paris is a living history and art museum with culinary flair. Hong Kong is condensed exoticism on the edge of the largest and longest running culture show in the world, China. Vancouver is a comfortable and easy to live in cosmopolitan city surrounded by some of the most spectacular scenery of any urban environment in the world.

Tokyo is different. Tokyo is a collection of villages, each different and each with its own personality. Overall, Tokyo is not a beautiful city. For the people who live there, however, and especially for most foreigners, it has a definite appeal. It is the *complete* city. Tokyo has everything you might be looking for in a metropolis, with the friendliness, politeness and honesty of a small village. Tokyo was to become my home for nine years.

I want to mention just one example of the friendliness and politeness that I encountered while living in Japan. In the 1990s, long after I had moved back to Canada, I was visiting Tokyo on business. I was getting ready to take the bus out to Narita Airport to return home. I wanted to buy flowers to send to Osaka, where I had been entertained at the home of a customer. I entered a flower shop to ask if that kind of service was available. The kind lady in the shop said no, but told me that another flower shop five minutes away did do this. She insisted that I leave my bags with her while I went to her competitor to buy the flowers I needed. Where else but in Tokyo?

Setting Language Goals, Tokyo 1971

Back in 1971 when I was first assigned to the Canadian Embassy in Tokyo I did not know what to expect. But I was determined to become fluent in Japanese, as I had promised my employer. My Chinese learning experience had allowed me to greatly improve my language learning methods and confidence. When I moved to Japan, I took these methods with me. I made a commitment to learn Japanese on my own, within six months. I would make every necessary sacrifice to achieve a breakthrough during this period. If I succeeded, I would then be able to live in Japanese, unlike the majority of Westerners who lived in English.

When my wife and I moved to Japan, we had one child and another on the way. My work at the Embassy was largely in English. Therefore, I had to work hard to surround myself with a Japanese language environment to learn from. Furthermore, in Japan I did not have the luxury of studying the language full time at my employer's expense, as had been the case in Hong Kong, nor had I studied the language in school as had been the case for French. I had to do it on my own while working full time.

Since the majority of foreigners were comfortable working and living in English, I knew that I had to force myself to live and work in Japanese as early as possible in order to avoid falling into the comfortable routine of "getting by" in English.

I had gained some initial exposure to Japanese while still in Hong Kong from good friends among the members of the Japanese consulate who were studying Chinese. One *Gaimusho* (Foreign Affairs) official was Mr. Koichi Kato, who subsequently became a leading Liberal Democratic politician. But my initial exposure to Japanese in Hong Kong was just a foretaste to get me interested.

My first six months of living in Japan formed my period of concentrated study, my make-or-break period. I had to find my own learning material and continue to develop my own language learning methods. I relied on bookstores to find content that I needed. This content was not as good as the content available for Chinese language study, and was certainly a far cry from the material that is available for studying any language today via the Internet.

Seeking Out Content

I knew that to progress in Japanese I had to expose myself to as much Japanese language content as possible. As soon as I could make out some of the meaning, I made a point of always listening to Japanese radio even though there was an English language radio station in Tokyo. I listened repeatedly to tapes, and read what I could. Unfortunately, there were not nearly as many readers with vocabulary lists available in Japanese as there had been for Chinese. When I think of how I struggled to find meaningful content to learn from, I envy today's learner for whom a vast world of interesting content is readily available to learn from with the appropriate learning system. Nowadays, more then ever before, it is possible to quickly progress from specially prepared beginner "textbook material" to the real language. The sooner you can get away from learner language and start to discover the real language, the faster you will progress.

You must be determined to find your own way to a new language, and be careful of teachers imposing their versions of the language on you. One evening I was driving home listening to Japanese Public Educational Radio (NHK) when I heard the following sounds coming from my radio, "Zey aa sayrazu, zey aa sayrazu." This went on for many minutes. I thought it was a Buddhist chant. Finally I realized that it was a radio English teacher with a heavy Japanese accent repeating the phrase "they are sailors." The pronunciation of the radio English instructor was marked by the influence of kana, a writing system based on syllables rather than individual sounds. Kana distorts the pronunciation of languages that were not designed to be written in Kana, and is an important obstacle faced by Japanese when trying to learn foreign languages. To make things worse, this radio program with its mindless repetitive mimicry of words was the opposite of meaningful content and therefore of little use. In a way, this reminded me of the French instruction I had in school. Today, English instruction in Japan is very advanced. There are many good schools and systems available, and there are young native speaker English teachers in every Japanese city and town. English teaching in Japan has progressed a great deal since the 1970s.

As my Japanese improved, I tried to vary the type of content to keep it interesting and to broaden my knowledge of the language. For example, when our family went on a tour of the Izu Peninsula, I took an audio version of Nobel Prize winner Kawabata Yasunari's novel *The Izu Dancers* along to listen to in the car. We retraced the route of the itinerant dancing troupe described in the novel while enjoying the picturesque mountain and ocean scenery of the region.

One of the most interesting tapes that I listened to was an NHK product called *The History of the Showa Era*. This consisted of re-broadcast live radio news from the period 1925 to 1945. Over time I was able to understand most of it. In my mind, I can still hear certain phrases from radio personalities announcing sports events or political or historical happenings from that period. Today, with the expanded production of audio books and e-books, there is a great deal of authentic content available in many languages to suit the interests of language learners.

While reading and repetitive listening are effective in becoming familiar with a new language, genuine interaction with native speakers is always the greatest stimulus and training ground for the learner. My closest colleague at the Canadian Embassy in Tokyo was the Japanese Commercial Officer, Mr. "Nick" Yazaki. He was a major help in my efforts to learn Japanese. He had the advantage, from my point of view, of being inclined to express himself in a most careful, painstaking and long-winded way. I imitated his pronunciation and his favourite turns of phrase. From the beginning, he supported me in my efforts to learn Japanese. He was an important influence on my learning. Finding a native speaker who is patient and supportive can be invaluable in learning a new language.

In time, I was able to hold up my end of most conversations. My conversation strategy was to try to keep what I had to say simple and well within my capabilities. I tried to avoid speaking quickly so that my thoughts did not run ahead of my language. This is easier said than done, however, and often I struggled to express myself. But it was all part of the learning process.

Is Japanese Difficult?

I am regularly asked by Japanese people if Japanese is the most difficult language to learn. They are disappointed if I do not agree that it is. But every language has its own unique difficulties, and with enough exposure all difficulties can be overcome. There is no unlearnable language. Certainly, the legions of young English language teachers who come to Japan to teach English are proof that Japanese presents no major problems for the person who wants to integrate with Japanese society. Many of these foreigners become good Japanese speakers. Young Japanese people are generally open and sociable and I often think these foreign teachers benefit more from their stay in Japan than their students who are trying to learn English.

A major obstacle to learning Japanese is the problem of the Chinese characters, or *Kanji* as they are called in Japanese. Many language learners can learn to speak well without reading, but it is easier to gain a feeling for the language if you can read it as you listen. Reading is a form of sensual appreciation of the language quite different from listening, and it strengthens your understanding of the language. Having learned most of the characters I needed from Chinese, I had an advantage. However, the pronunciation in Japanese can be a problem. Unlike Chinese, there are often several ways to pronounce the same characters. The meaning of Chinese characters in Japanese can sometimes be different from the meaning in Chinese.

I had to design my own learning program based on my interests and abilities. This is easily done in today's digital age but was very difficult to do when I lived in Tokyo. Knowing the Kanji characters, at least in Chinese, I concentrated on Japanese content that was weighted towards Chinese characters, such as the newspapers and the radio news, and then progressed to more day-to-day conversation. I was able to conduct business in Japanese fairly soon, but did not understand television soap operas until later.

Living in a Japanese environment and reading the Japanese newspapers daily trained my mind to read characters. I observed that my ability to read Chinese improved while I was in Japan, although I essentially never read Chinese. I think that my ability to speak Chinese also improved because my brain was becoming even more capable of processing different languages. Certainly, learning new languages has never crowded out previously learned languages or confused me.

The relationship between writing systems and the brain is interesting and illustrates the many sided nature of language learning. According to Robert Ornstein in *The Right Mind*:

Almost all pictographic systems [of writing] favor a vertical layout, while most phonographic systems are horizontal. And out of several hundred phonographic systems that have vowels, almost all are written toward the right, while of over fifty languages that do not have any signs for vowels, all are written to the left. This strongly suggests that there is a good reason for the connection between type of system and direction. And the most likely candidate is that our eyes and brain work in different ways depending on what sorts of scripts they are reading. It is likely that the culture one encounters at birth and first few years affects the way the hemispheres are organized

The Greeks, as well as just about everybody else in the world, developed their alphabet from the Phoenician alphabet. By mid-700s BC, the new Greek alphabet was in use but being written from right to left in the same way as its parent. Within a hundred and fifty years or so it was written in boustrophedon, referring to the route an ox plows a field-alternately right to left and left to right. But by about 550 BC it had settled down into the familiar left to right.

Aside from the writing system, another early obstacle I found in Japanese was the similarity of the sounds. This is a common reaction when starting a new language, but Japanese has, in fact, fewer different sounds than most languages. Vocabulary acquisition was slow at first. This problem disappeared as I got used to seeing and hearing words in their natural contexts. Difficulties encountered at the early stages in language learning can be discouraging. However, consistent exposure and an open mind will gradually allow you to overcome these problems.

Polite Language

Perhaps the most unique aspect of Japanese is the use of different words and sentence structures for different social situations. No language I have learned has such a difference of vocabulary and structure depending on whether you are talking casually to a friend, to a subordinate, or very formally to a "senior" person. Just the word "I" has at least three commonly used forms, *watakushi, boku* and *ore*, and the same is true for "you" and the other pronouns.

To master these distinctions you must be involved often in social situations that require you to use them correctly. Just explaining the logic behind language patterns will not enable you to master them. You have to become a little bit Japanese in your mentality before you can switch on polite or casual language depending on the social setting. This requires considerable exposure, either in real life situations or through listening to appropriate material in recorded form. It also requires you to accept the culture.

Until I mastered the different levels of politeness, I simply spoke neutral Japanese. In fact, to a large extent I still do. I think it is important not to try to be either too colloquial or too formal when speaking a foreign language. It is normally not expected of a foreigner. Nor is total mastery of the politeness levels necessary for communication. Fully understanding the nuances of polite words and phrases requires a very advanced level of cultural sensitivity that cannot be forced, but will develop naturally over time.

Apparently the sentence structure of Japanese is of North Asian origin and therefore similar to Korean. Much of the original vocabulary is, according to some experts, vaguely related to Polynesian languages and comes from the Jomon people who settled in Japan starting 20,000 years ago. The Jomon were hunter-gatherers who lived in Japan before different waves of North Asian immigrants, called Yayoi people, brought rice culture and the influence of their language to Japan starting around 300 BC. Incidentally, the Jomon people may have been the first in the world to develop pottery— over 10,000 years ago.

The Chinese writing system was introduced to Japan just over 1,500 years ago, along with many Chinese words, Chinese technology and the Buddhist religion. The magnificent wooden structures found in Nara and Kyoto include the oldest and largest wooden buildings in the world. The techniques used in construction are the best preserved and most outstanding examples of Chinese wood building technology, which dates back to the original Yellow River civilization.

In recent times, the Japanese language has accepted many foreign borrowed words, especially from English. Japanese is a rich amalgam of many influences. Knowledge of the Chinese characters is an advantage to a foreigner learning Japanese, and the grammatical structure of Japanese is similar to Korean. So neighboring Asian people have an advantage in learning Japanese. However, the attitude of the learner is a more important factor than geographic or genetic proximity. I have met many foreigners from other parts of the world who have a positive attitude and excel at spoken Japanese.

At a time when I was already fluent in Japanese, my wife, who looks Asian, still could not speak Japanese very well. Often we had triangular conversations with Japanese people in public places. I spoke Japanese, and the Japanese person replied to my wife. The Japanese person could not accept the fact that the Western face, not the Asian face, was the one actually speaking Japanese.

In a similar vein, years later in Canada, an older Japanese lady made the following observation about a young child of mixed Japanese-Caucasian parents who was late in starting to talk. "Of course he is slow, since Japanese people have trouble speaking English!"

I hear Caucasians marvel that a Caucasian can learn an Asian language even though we are familiar with second generation Canadians of Asian origin who are native speakers of English. How many times have I heard Chinese people say that English is impossible to learn because Chinese culture is so different from English? This kind of cultural preconception is just another obstacle to proper language learning and needs to be discarded. I am convinced that anyone, of whatever culture or background, and of whatever age, can learn any language if they commit to doing so.

A Westerner visiting or living in Japan who will only eat "meat and potatoes" and does not enjoy sushi will usually not be successful in learning Japanese. Similarly, Japanese people who will only travel abroad in groups and will only eat familiar food are unlikely to be successful in learning other foreign languages, no matter how much time they spend trying. Learning a language is like traveling. Both activities are an adventure. There is no point in traveling abroad and acting like you stayed at home.

Japan Incorporated

Japan in the 1970s and early 1980s was different from today's Japan. It was a less open society.

During the first four years of my stay in Japan I was First Secretary at the Canadian Embassy. During this time I was involved in initiating a program to introduce the North American platform frame wood building system to Japan. This program met the objectives of the Japanese Ministry of Construction, which was concerned about the projected lack of carpenters trained in the demanding traditional Japanese building system. This was a time of rapid improvement in living standards and a high annual level of house construction.

I enjoyed my stint at the Embassy because of my close involvement with my Japanese counterparts, especially those like the Ministry of Construction officials and the members of the Tokyo Young Lumbermen's Association who participated in the introduction of the new wood frame building system. On the other hand, the social obligations of the diplomatic service, the frequent evening cocktail parties and entertainment which ate into my private life, were less enjoyable.

At the end of my Embassy posting in October 1974, despite vague plans to return to University to do Asian Studies, I was recruited by Seaboard Lumber Sales, a leading Canadian forest products company, to set up a subsidiary company in Tokyo. I would never have been given this opportunity had I not learned Japanese. I worked in the forest industry in Japan from 1974 to 1977 for Seaboard and then returned to Vancouver with my family. We returned to Japan for a further two years, from 1981 to 1982, on behalf of another major Canadian forest products company, MacMillan Bloedel Ltd.

This was a period when Japan, although very pleased to export large amounts of manufactured goods, was only slowly and reluctantly opening up its market to imports, despite the efforts of foreign exporters and Japanese people involved in import. As the person in charge of MacMillan Bloedel's operations in Asia, I was responsible for marketing paper and pulp as well as lumber. I occasionally encountered trade barriers.

The paper industry in Japan was a tightly knit community of users, producers and government officials. It was particularly difficult for our Japanese employees to be seen promoting Canadian paper in competition with Japanese producers. It was almost considered unpatriotic. A famous book, *The Day We Ran Out of Paper*, was written in 1981 under a pseudonym by an official of MITI (the Japanese Ministry of International Trade and Industry). The message of this book was that a Japanese newspaper publisher importing foreign newsprint paper was selling out freedom of speech to a foreign conspiracy. Times have changed now, and Japanese paper companies themselves have built paper mills in many countries of the world, including Canada.

In the 1980s, under trade liberalization pressure from the United States, the Japanese Telephone Company (NTT) allowed foreign paper producers to bid for the telephone directory paper business. Our company was the first foreign supplier to pass the quality testing. That was the easy part. It was much more difficult to deal with the cozy relationships between Japanese suppliers and customers, often described by the term "Japan Incorporated."

The Japanese paper producers, who were our competitors, had retired senior executives of NTT, our common customer, on their Boards of Directors. Furthermore, we had to deal through a "fixer" agency company owned and run by retired employees of NTT. The printing companies were also owned and run by ex-employees of NTT. My ability to read and speak Japanese helped me navigate this world of complex relationships and create a market for our Canadian paper products.

The Japanese paper market was dominated by a small number of large producers and users and, therefore, it was easy for semi-monopolistic trading practices to become established. The lumber trade, however, was different. It consisted of a large number of traditionally minded lumber retailers, wholesalers and homebuilders. Paradoxically, because of the larger number of participants, the traditional Japanese lumber sector was more open than the modern and sophisticated paper sector.

My relationship with the Japanese lumber trade was to become a dominant experience in my life. I was able to experience first-hand the Japanese love of nature and their pursuit of excellence in product design and manufacture. Their respect for their traditional house building system and the skills of the carpenter, and their appreciation and understanding of wood, have all had a profound and lasting impact on me.

To sit in a traditional Japanese room with the fragrance of Hinoki cypress still emanating from the woodwork, facing the Tokonoma or alcove where a simple scroll is hanging, while sipping hot sake and waiting for a dish of delicious sashimi to be brought in, is but one of the pleasures of having been initiated to Japanese culture. There is a sense of perfection about the whole experience, from the way the fish was cut, to the design of the porcelain, to the selection of just the right piece of wood for each piece of joinery in the room.

In English there is an expression, " If something is worth doing, it is worth doing well." Probably similar expressions exist in all languages. However, nowhere is this spirit put into practice more thoroughly than in Japan. Japanese literature has many stories of people from samurais to sword-makers to simple potters who dedicated their lives to their craft. This spirit helped Japan become a world leader in manufacturing, and forced the American car industry to change its practices and improve its quality standards.

The Japanese desire for excellence found a ready application in modern statistics-based quality control procedures. When we sold lumber to large industrialized house manufacturers we were obliged to provide details on all aspects of our production process that could be measured. At first we resisted these demands for quality measurement. Soon we realized that only with measurement of the key input factors and output results was it possible to reduce problems and improve performance. Our company, and our supplying sawmills, all benefited from these demands from our Japanese customers.

Statistical measurement can be important in many fields of activity, and especially in language learning, as I will explain later.

Fitting In

I learned many things in my nine years of living in Japan and over 30 years of doing business there. The Japanese way of communicating was one of them. Japanese people generally spend more time observing and less time talking than the average North American, who instead is usually more eager to tell his side of the story. The Japanese also prefer to avoid confrontation and are certainly not eager to engage in great arguments based on the fine points of logic, a practice more dear to the French. So to do business in Japan you have to learn to listen. The more you talk, the less you will hear and the less you will learn about the interests and intentions of your Japanese counterpart. Like good quality control, learning to be a listener is not a bad habit to acquire, regardless of your culture.

I also made it a habit to say anything important in a business negotiation directly in Japanese. Nuances and intentions are easily lost in translation. With very few exceptions, I was never confident that my true meaning was understood unless I expressed it myself in Japanese. Whenever I am in a foreign language environment, I decide who speaks whose language better, my counterpart or me. If it is me, then I make sure I use my counterpart's language to avoid misunderstandings.

Like many people in the world, the Japanese pride themselves on their unique culture. To some extent different cultures are unique and yet they are connected to each other at the same time. When we lived in Japan it was common for the Japanese to speak of themselves as having an "island mentality". While the Japanese are amongst the best educated people in the world, with a surprisingly wide range of interests and knowledge in food, music, literature and history, there were many people who were conservative and protective of what they considered their unique ways. When my family and I lived in Japan we had to make the effort to fit in, recognizing that there would be limits to our ability to penetrate the inner "we" of Japan. We could never be Japanese. Yet people were generally hospitable and friendly.

Japanese culture has a refined esthetic tradition, which, although inspired by many Chinese influences, is uniquely Japanese in its expression. Even in busy modern Japan, one frequently comes across islands of understated serenity in gardens, Buddhist temples, Shinto shrines or even private homes. The conviviality of eating a Japanese meal seated on a tatami mat is something I never grow tired of. Now that Japanese cuisine has become truly international, Carmen and I always feel nostalgic when we are able to enjoy Japanese food in a truly Japanese atmosphere elsewhere in the world.

Soon after establishing the Japanese subsidiary of Seaboard Lumber Sales Ltd. in 1975, my president came out for his first visit to Japan. I decided I would offer him a traditional geisha party at a traditional Japanese inn at a hot spring resort outside of Tokyo. Geishas are ladies who are highly trained in music, conversation, and the art of entertainment.

Two geishas were to come to our room at six o'clock. My president and I took our Japanese bath and put on our Japanese robes for dinner. My president was in great spirits as he anticipated the evening, putting on his favourite eau de cologne. We really did not know what to expect. At six, there was a gentle knock on the wooden door which gradually slid open. The first geisha shuffled into the room. She must have been sixty years old! Her partner then came in and she seemed even older. Needless to say neither one of the geishas spoke English. I could sense the disappointment on the face of my president, and probably the geishas felt that we were expecting younger entertainers. However, we had a delightful evening. Those two ladies were wonderful. They skillfully communicated their art to my president, even though they spoke no English. Of course I helped with translation, but I am sure they would have managed without me.

Geisha parties or traditional Japanese meals are best enjoyed at Japanese inns. There, guests can enjoy a piping hot Japanese bath before dining. These baths are one of the delights of Japanese culture. You sit on a low stool to wash yourself before soaking in water that can be as hot as 45 degrees. After the bath you wear a Japanese yukata or robe. Unfortunately long-legged Westerners have trouble keeping themselves appropriately covered in these robes, especially when trying to sit on a Japanese tatami mat floor. At one such party in the early 1980s, the president of MacMillan Bloedel, who is over six feet tall, had on a pair of underpants with a red pattern. It was impossible for him to arrange his legs in such a way that the ever-observant geishas could not notice the interesting pattern on his underpants. Immediately, amidst much laughter, he was given the name "akapan" or red pants, by one of the geishas. The name followed him back to Vancouver!

I was lucky enough to enjoy quite a few geisha parties in the 1970s, but this tradition seems to have become much less common in the last twenty years. Nevertheless, the hospitality shown to me and many visiting Canadians was always generous and genuine, and offered simply because we came from so far away. Today, whenever I have an opportunity to reciprocate hospitality to Japanese visitors to Vancouver, I am only too happy to do so.

I often encountered the conservatism of Japanese society when trying to promote the import of new products. At times I went against established practices to achieve the objectives of my company. This often upset our Japanese counterparts. I was once described as the "Kaufmann Typhoon" in a lumber trade newspaper. However, I always felt that Japanese business people were able to maintain an attitude of respect, even when disagreeing on substantive issues. Mutual respect is a fundamental part of the mood of Japanese society, and a large reason for their social cohesion and success.

It is important to participate in the culture of a country, in order to be in a state of mind to absorb the language. Not all encounters are pleasant or welcoming, but you have to persevere. Sometimes you meet resistance because you are a foreigner. This phenomenon is not unique to any culture, and can happen at any time. But most encounters will be pleasant and memorable.

One of my proudest moments in Japan was when I participated in the *Kiba Matsuri*, or Wood Market Festival. I was a member of one of many groups of young men wearing white shorts or loin cloth, a cotton *happi* coat and a *hachimaki* wrapped around my forehead. We carried heavy wooden shrines through Tokyo's streets from morning to night, drinking sake and getting showered with water by the onlookers. We shouted *Wasshoi* every time the heavy wooden shrine was thrown up into the air and caught again. Since I was taller than the other men, I either had to carry a disproportionate share of the load or constantly bend my knees. I guess I did a little of both from 5:30 in the morning until 3:30 in the afternoon. That night I could hardly crawl into bed, I was so tired and sore.

I often noticed that some foreigners who studied Japanese reached the peak of their language capability at the end of their period of language learning. Once launched into Japanese working life, they reverted back to living in English and their Japanese skills deteriorated. They never pushed themselves far enough to make living and working in Japanese seem natural for them. I deliberately took a different approach. This did not mean that I could not also live in English with other Canadians, it just meant that I had created another option for myself, that of living in Japanese.

Many foreign diplomats and businesspeople belonged to the Tokyo American club, which had a large swimming pool, tennis courts and elegant facilities. We belonged to a small Japanese tennis club called Hokuyu, (meaning Northern friend, perhaps appropriately named for a Canadian) with an old wooden clubhouse and kerosene stove for the colder days of winter. There, Carmen and I would play tennis most weekends, while our two boys played in the neighbouring schoolyard until they got bored and wanted to go home. We did not need to reserve a court, but just showed up. We would always be asked to join a game. While we waited in the clubhouse watching others play, we had ample opportunity to practice our Japanese. I remember one small Japanese gentlemen, at least twenty years older and fifteen kilograms lighter than me, who would always ask me to play. I just could not beat him.

The tendency for us to be most comfortable in our own cultural community is normal; however, it is no help to language learning. Once you really commit to the local language and make more local friends and professional acquaintances, the differences between people become less obvious than the similarities. I thoroughly enjoyed my nine-year stay in Japan. I came away with a profound appreciation for Japanese culture and the refinement that the Japanese bring to so many aspects of daily human activities.

I am aware of cultural differences between people, just as I notice differences of personality between individuals. Yet my understanding of the essential similarity of all individual human beings was only confirmed during my nine years in Japan. Above all, every human being is an individual, with hopes and fears and ambitions. We seek comfort from belonging to communities, whether local, national or religious. However, an even greater sense of comfort is available to those of us who recognize that, as individuals, we are all equal members of the human family.

In Japan today, the "island mentality" is giving way to a "world citizen mentality" amongst young people. My son, Mark, played professional hockey in Japan for three years. He found easy friendship with his Japanese teammates, whether on the ice or relaxing after hours, and his Japanese has become quite fluent. Nowadays it is quite common to find young Japanese people living and working abroad in every corner of the world, where they have become fluent in the local language.

Japan is facing many economic difficulties today. The traditional hierarchical structure of Japanese society has inhibited the input of the younger generation towards solving these problems. This will likely change. In what Kennichi Ohmae, a leading Japanese thinker, calls "the modern borderless world," increased knowledge of foreign languages will ensure a greater diversity of perspectives on issues affecting Japanese society.

Exploring Languages at Home

Without going outside, you may know the whole world.
Without looking through the window,
you may see the ways of heaven.
– Laozi

It is always easiest to learn a language when you are living in a society that speaks that language if you take advantage of the opportunities that surround you. However, a new language in the real world can be difficult to understand. People may talk too quickly or use words that even the intermediate non-native speaker does not understand. You may feel hesitant in certain situations because you are not fluent. This can be stressful.

In these cases I have always found it useful to create my own world of language, a world of meaningful language content for me to listen to or read without pressure. Until I mastered Japanese, and even as I was living and working in Japanese, I still sought out advanced Japanese readers with meaningful content and vocabulary lists to read. I also listened repetitively to interesting tapes to gain greater confidence in using certain phrases and words.

I still listen to interesting material in languages that I speak fluently. I take advantage of time that is available while driving or exercising or doing chores around the house. There is an increasing availability of high quality audio books which can be easily enjoyed using the latest in portable listening technology.

As mentioned earlier, electronic texts have many advantages for the language learner. There are already a host of language learning products that take advantage of the interactive features of e-text. I regularly enjoy reading in foreign languages on the Internet. I use The Linguist system to increase my vocabulary in these languages and to save many of these articles as part of my ever-growing language library.

In situations where you are studying a new language away from the native speaking environment, it becomes essential to create this personal language world. This is what I have done in Vancouver over the last twenty years as I sought to improve my knowledge of languages that I had been exposed to earlier but could not speak.

A World Apart

When I lived in Hong Kong I was not in a Mandarin speaking environment, but I listened to and read a limited number of texts: history and cultural books, modern literature, and tapes of comic dialogues. These became like old friends and provided the core of the vocabulary and phrasing that I needed to use in my communication.

Communicating with this imaginary world was easier than communicating with the real world, since it was readily available and under my control. This friendly world of my own exploration was a great source of strength in preparation for the real test of communicating with native speakers.

> **In 1512, Niccolo Machiavelli was briefly imprisoned and tortured by the Medici family, then withdrew to a simple country house outside Florence. During the day he talked and played cards with the local people, but at night he changed into formal clothes and withdrew into his study. There he communicated with the ancient historians through books, and wrote one of the classics of Western literature, *The Prince*. Machiavelli is an example of how we can communicate with a culture through reading or listening, even if we do not have daily personal contact with the people.**

While living in Vancouver well past the age of forty, I was able to make great advances on the learning I had begun in German, Swedish and Italian. I had some previous exposure, but certainly did not have fluency or confidence. For each language, I had to commit myself to a concentrated period of listening to comprehensible audio material and reading texts with vocabulary lists.

At my home, I have at least fifty readers for German, Italian, Spanish, and Swedish. I purchased these readers because they all have vocabulary lists so that I could avoid using dictionaries. Unfortunately, much of the content of these readers was uninteresting to me, but it was the only content that I could find.

What I was only able to do through great effort is made easier and more effective today. Using modern technology, vast amounts of content can be turned into accessible learning material. The virtual explosion of high quality audio books in many languages represents an exciting opportunity for enjoyment and learning. We are starting to see audio magazines where you can hear and read the same content. A system like The Linguist makes it possible for learners to access this real content and learn from it while enjoying the adventure of communicating with a foreign language and culture. You can literally seek out any content that is of interest to you, and learn the language from it. The independent learner is more independent than ever before. I am now adding delightful audio books in many languages to my original stock of books and cassettes.

German

My ability in German is considered good by native speakers and I have no difficulty in conversation, or in understanding radio and newspapers. Although I had exposure to German in my younger days at home, while working on a German ship and while working on construction in Vienna, I really could not carry on a conversation. In November 1986, I decided to spend the month learning German.

I went to many secondhand bookstores in Vancouver looking for reading books in the German language which had vocabulary lists. I must have bought about ten or fifteen of such books, as well as various cassette tape products in German. The readers were full of the scribblings of the people who had used them before. For one month I read and listened to tapes in German, with the help of vocabulary lists. Of course I achieved a dramatic improvement in my German. I was subsequently able to improve on this during visits to Germany. But it was hard work.

In German, the nouns have three genders. Word endings change depending on case. This is very hard to master in speech. Only repetitive listening has enabled me to cope with this difficulty, not explanations and lists. I just speak German the way I hear it and hope for the best. My German is natural and fluent, but I am resigned to the fact that I am not perfect in German grammar.

I never had to pass a test in German, but I have done business in that language. I have also traveled to the wonderful medieval towns of Germany, sat down in restaurants and engaged the locals in lengthy conversations in German. I know that I frequently get my genders and cases wrong. It has not held me back. On the other hand, I know that to improve my grammar I just have to listen and read more, and occasionally refer to grammar texts to reinforce what I am experiencing in the real language. The isolated study of cases and genders, without a lot of language exposure, will not enable me to improve my grammar in real situations.

Italian

Italian is relatively easy for someone familiar with Spanish and French. Concentrated listening to tapes and reading soon brought my Italian up to a usable level. Unfortunately I have too little opportunity to use it, but I always enjoy watching an Italian movie and being able to understand what is said. I also intend to buy more Italian e-books and audio books when I have the time.

Italian is known as the language of music and love. While Italian may have the reputation of being an exceptionally beautiful language, I find that all languages are beautiful when I study them and start to understand them. When any language is well spoken, it has its own elegance and beauty. I always appreciate hearing people speak a language well, with the appropriate choice of words and with clarity, and with reference to the culture and history of that language.

> It is impossible to study Italian without thinking of the enormous cultural contribution of Italy to Europe and the world. But Italy was as much a conduit of culture as a creator. It was the influence of Greece, itself stimulated by other more ancient Mediterranean cultures, that was Rome's great teacher. The Romans respected Greek culture and in their myth of origin they try to impute their ancestry back to Aeneas of Troy. (This myth, like so many myths of origin, is not true.)
>
> The legacy of Rome's law and literature and its great public works have profoundly marked Western civilization. Long after the collapse of the Roman Empire, the genius of Italian culture again flourished in various city-states. As always in history, the stimulus of foreign contact was paramount. Venice achieved its splendour because of its dominance of the sea and contacts with Byzantium and the East. Similarly the involvement of Italian cities like Genoa and the cities of Tuscany in foreign trade, including trade with the Muslim world, contributed to their rapid growth in the early Middle Ages, and eventually led to the Italian Renaissance.

Cantonese

It was after the age of fifty in Vancouver that I decided to really work on Cantonese, since so many people in Vancouver speak that language. I had always heard some Cantonese when I was with my wife's Chinese relatives. However, my ability did not go far beyond ordering food in a restaurant, and even there I made mistakes.

I am never shy about using what little language knowledge I have. Once in a restaurant when I wanted to order a dozen spring rolls or *chun gyun*, I ordered a dozen *chun doi* or "spring bags." In Chinese the word *chun* means spring, and has the connotation of sex. (I find that a very poetic association.) Unfortunately for me, *chun doi* or spring bags refers to the male sex organ and not to an item of food. After the initial shock at what I had said subsided, there was laughter all around.

My wife grew up speaking Cantonese. However, she and I always spoke English at home and we were not about to change the habits of thirty years. I was able to read the Chinese newspaper in Mandarin but could not pronounce the characters in Cantonese. I enlisted the help of my friend, the Cantonese speaking Vancouver journalist Gabriel Yiu, but really did not make progress.

I suppose I understood about ten percent of what was said in conversation or on the radio. I believe a person needs to understand well over ninety percent of most situations to be considered fluent. I had a long way to go. The problem was that I had a bad attitude. Subconsciously, I felt that the pronunciation, with nine tones, was simply too difficult. I also felt that Mandarin, the national language, was good enough and that I really did not need Cantonese. I did not have commitment.

I started searching Chinese bookstores in Vancouver for Cantonese learning material. I found a book that amounted to a breakthrough. This book demystified the issue of the nine tones of Cantonese. This system emphatically stated that six tones were enough. This seemed very sensible to me since I felt I could not even get six tones right and would still be able to communicate adequately. In addition, the author showed that these same tones existed in English, not to distinguish the meaning of words, but to provide emphasis in sentences. I suddenly realized that the phenomenon of all these tones was already familiar to me from English. I had been a prisoner of my fear of the tones. Now the obstacle of the tones was removed and the doors opened.

Next, I needed material to listen to. I asked people to tape simple content for me that I listened to over and over. Then I bought a Minidisc player, which is a truly revolutionary tool for the language learner. It can record from radio or television as well as download from a computer. It can record your own voice and store a great deal of material. Yet it is light to carry and the sound quality is outstanding.

I soon started recording Cantonese radio programs, including talk show programs. As my Cantonese improved, I started to phone in to the Cantonese radio talk shows to offer my opinions on different subjects. I recorded this all and compared myself to the native speaker announcers. I believe the Minidisc recorder enabled me to achieve a degree of concentration in my learning that contributed to my breakthrough in acquiring Cantonese. Unfortunately, I have not been able to find electronic texts in Cantonese which correspond to the audio material that is available. I am sure this will come and that it will facilitate the learning of Cantonese.

By concentrating on content that I enjoyed listening to, and with my knowledge of Mandarin to help me, my comprehension gradually improved. This reinforced all my previous experiences with language learning. It pointed out once again the crucial role of the learner in achieving success, and the importance of finding interesting material. Also, my success at Cantonese confirmed to me that age is no barrier to effective language learning, if the learner is prepared to make the commitment.

While I am not totally fluent, I am able to carry on a conversation, even to the point of phoning in to radio talk shows. My six-month period of greatest effort is now behind me, and I will continue to improve just by listening to the radio and meeting with people. I recently spent a few days in Shen Zhen and Guang Zhou (Canton) after an absence of twenty years. Of course I was amazed at the changes in those places. I thoroughly enjoyed being able to speak Cantonese with people that I met, which greatly added to the enjoyment of my visit.

I had to work hard to learn languages. I had to search for readers with word lists. The content was not always interesting and did not come with audio tapes. It took a lot of effort to build up my personal language world in these different languages. It is much easier to create your language learning world today. At a website like The Linguist, it is possible to make available a limitless variety of content on different subjects in different languages for a learner to choose from. This content can consist of both audio files and digital text files. The learner can download files, listen and read, and save words and phrases for later review. Today there are powerful hand-held computers which operate as e-book readers and MP3 players. New wireless technology means that people are already able to connect to the Internet wirelessly in offices, hotels, airports, train stations or coffee shops. The opportunity to use every free minute to study subjects of interest will make language learning more flexible, more customized, more intense and yet more enjoyable.

With the Internet, the self-study of languages need not be such a lonely task. The Internet makes it possible to have flexible interaction with coaches as required. In addition, it is possible to connect with other language learners to practice language or simply to share experiences. I am looking forward to learning more languages myself, and continuing to upgrade skills in the languages that I already speak.

Language and International Business

You never step in the same river twice, for fresh waters are ever flowing in upon you.
– Heraclitus, 6th century BC

In June 1987, I started my own company in lumber export. For six months my wife and I worked out of the basement of our home with a fax machine and a phone. I traveled thousands of kilometres by car in Western Canada. I traveled tens of thousands of kilometres by air to Japan and Europe. Fifteen years later we have offices in Vancouver, Northern Alberta, Sweden and Japan, and a well established international trading business. I could not have done this without my knowledge of languages.

Admittedly, success in business life does not depend solely on language skills. There are countless examples of outstanding business people who are able to get by only speaking their first language, especially when that language is English. However, being a linguist can help in many ways, and it certainly helped me.

Opportunity

Throughout our lives we are surrounded by opportunities. It is only by being active and acquiring knowledge that we are able to see these opportunities and to take advantage of them. In my case it was my willingness to learn languages that created my opportunities.

Although I had already learned two languages in addition to English, it was my move to Japan, and the subsequent acquisition of the Japanese language, that made a major difference to my life. Speaking Japanese, I was able to create good personal contacts in the Japanese business community. For this reason I was later hired by two of the major Canadian lumber exporting companies, on two separate occasions, to run their Asian marketing operations. This eventually resulted in me starting my own company, whereby I was able to achieve a certain degree of financial independence.

I do not know what path I would have followed if I had gone to Beijing after all. No doubt I would have become more fluent in Chinese. I might still be in the diplomatic service or in the academic field or perhaps other opportunities would have come along. But pursuing languages was like a net for me, allowing me to catch opportunities that would otherwise have passed me by.

One example occurred in 1981. As President of MacMillan Bloedel Asia Ltd., based in Tokyo, I was back in Vancouver on a business trip. M. Bernard Guillemette, an important customer from France, was also visiting Vancouver at the same time. I was the only marketing person available at MacMillan Bloedel who spoke French. Even though I was responsible for the Far East, I ended up accompanying M. Guillemette for a whole day visiting our sawmills. From that day, we formed a lasting friendship.

Many years later, Guillemette et Cie. became my own company's best customer in Europe and has remained so. What is more, in October 1992 I took part in Bernard Guillemette's sixty-fifth birthday party in Paris, a gala dinner on a boat floating down the Seine. At that dinner I met another guest, Mr. Christer Johansson, President of Vida Timber of Sweden. We struck up a friendship which also continues to this day. Within four months of meeting Mr. Johansson, fluctuations in international currencies made European lumber competitive in Japan. Working with Vida, our company was among the first exporters of lumber from Sweden to Japan. Vida has subsequently grown to become one of the largest lumber producers in Sweden and is our main supplier to Japan from Europe. These relationships were partly the result of luck, but could not have been achieved without my knowledge of French and Swedish, not to mention Japanese.

When I started my own company, my main idea was to focus on producing the special lumber sizes used in the Japanese manufactured house industry. Not a particularly brilliant idea, perhaps, but one that made sense at that time.

Because I had close relations with various people in the Japanese wood industry I had a good understanding of the trends in the market. I also was confident that some of my friends and contacts would trust me in my new venture. It was my relationship with these people, the result of my fluency in Japanese, that created this opportunity for me.

Even though our company was a newcomer with no history of meeting commitments, I was able to obtain the support of the world's largest private sector home manufacturer, Sekisui House Limited, to supply their wooden structural housing components. This relationship was to prove instrumental to the future success of my new company. We benefited from our relationship with Sekisui both directly and indirectly, because of what we learned and were able to apply to relationships in Japan with large house building companies such as Sekisui Chemical, Sumitomo Forestry, as well as other distributors and home builders.

I am convinced that I would not have been given this opportunity by Sekisui had I not been able to speak Japanese. During the period that we supplied Sekisui we had an intense collaboration with Sekisui sales and technical people both in head office and at their manufacturing plants. Their quality and delivery demands were strict. There had to be mutual confidence and an ability to deal with problems which occasionally arose. My company grew to be their largest wood supplier in the early 1990s and we were made to feel a part of their family of suppliers. This relationship had an unexpected impact on the small community of Manning, Alberta in Northern Canada.

The town of Manning, in Northern Alberta, is surrounded by large farms and bison ranches. In every direction, however, these fields soon give way to the vast boreal forest, home to bears, wolves, moose and other wildlife, as well as oil and gas exploration and forest industry activity. In the winter, in this land of the northern lights, the thermometer can stay under 40 below zero for weeks at a time. Summers, however, are sunny and warm. In June of 1994 Mr. Isao Okui, the fluently bilingual President of Sekisui House and one of the most highly respected business leaders in Japan, visited this small remote town to participate in the official opening of a new sawmill, Manning Diversified Forest Products. Sekisui House, together with my small company, several local business people, and an aboriginal settlement 200 kilometers north of Manning were equal partners in this new venture, which was to prove a success for the townspeople and for the investors. People of different backgrounds had come together for a common purpose. In a small way this was a long-term consequence of my language ability.

Not all my dealings in Japan were with large companies. My friend, Mr. Hiromi Higuma, the President of a medium sized regional wholesaler called the Bungohama Company, agreed immediately over a sushi lunch to switch his purchasing of traditional Japanese lumber components to my company, based on a mutual trust that had developed between us over the previous ten years. These relationships depended on my fluency in Japanese and could not have been achieved in English. These international relationships have continued over the years and are amongst the greatest rewards of international business.

Even with my Canadian suppliers, language was a positive factor in building trust. My two most important Canadian partners are both linguists in their own way.

Mr. Norm Boucher, President of Manning Diversified Forest Products Ltd., is a dynamic and self-reliant leader of the lumber industry in Alberta. He is originally from Quebec and speaks French. Even though we conduct most of our business in English, our ability to communicate in French created an additional degree of mutual understanding and trust. Norm grew up in the harsh environment of Northern Alberta to which he is still attached today. He likes to tell the story of how tough his childhood was. As a young boy on winter mornings, he would have to go out to a frozen lake in minus thirty degree celsius weather and make a hole in the ice to fetch water for the family. On his way back he had to check the rabbit traps for the dinner stew. Once, during a visit to Japan in the 1990s, we were at a sumptuous dinner of Japanese food. Norm was struggling to eat with the unfamiliar chopsticks. With his characteristic sense of humour he told our Japanese hosts that when he was growing up his family was poor and had to survive on rabbit meat but at least they could afford a fork!

Mr. Ben Sawatzky has been my partner in developing the Japanese market. He is President of Spruceland Millworks Ltd. and an outstanding business leader. He is quick to decide what to do, and then follows his decision through to completion. He started with one employee and now employs one hundred fifty people in three plants. In addition, he owns several ranches and has built a private school. Ben speaks German and Spanish as well as English. We have traveled together in Germany and Spain, and our interest in languages has given us something in common beyond our business dealings.

Ben always wanted to learn Japanese so he could join in the conversation with our Japanese customers. He studied Japanese off and on but not consistently. Once in Sendai at a meal hosted by Japanese customers, he took advantage of the fact that I had gone to the bathroom to try out his language. Ben always speaks in a strong voice. He wanted to say that the meal was "oishikatta" meaning "was delicious" but he confused the past tense with the negative and told our host in his usual forceful way that the meal was "oishiku arimasen" meaning "not good." In language, a little knowledge can be a dangerous thing!

Norm Boucher and Ben Sawatzky became partners in our successful sawmill venture in Northern Alberta.

Success

To succeed in any endeavour requires enthusiasm and hard work. This is true for an employee, for an entrepreneur and for someone studying languages. This enthusiasm gives you the energy to work hard to overcome obstacles and to take advantage of opportunities. I have worked with many people who had enthusiasm and were effective in their work. They were not all linguists, but they had the knowledge and ability that transcends language barriers. These kinds of people exist in every culture and language group. Such people can also become good linguists if they are motivated to do so.

But language is not a condition of success in business, just an enhancer. If you are a good business person, the ability to communicate in other languages can make you more effective. In business, you need credibility. People have to trust you. Business is dependent on a network of people: colleagues, employees, bosses, customers, suppliers, advisors, friends and others on whom you can rely and who are prepared to rely on you. If you are not trustworthy, reliable and effective at what you do, speaking foreign languages will not help you. I believe it was Voltaire who said of a certain French nobleman that he spoke six languages and had nothing to say in any of them.

However, speaking a foreign language fluently can be invaluable in building relationships of trust. You need not speak like a native speaker, but you need to be comfortably fluent. You need to be able to communicate without struggling and your counterpart needs to feel comfortable communicating with you in the language. This is the professional level of language competence that is required for international business. To achieve this professional level requires a commitment to reading and listening to a great deal of relevant content, the systematic study and use of new words and phrases, as well as a willingness to communicate regularly in the new language as your proficiency improves.

The language learning opportunities available with new information technology should be of particular interest to business people. It is possible to access learning material at the office, while traveling, or just about anywhere. Busy modern people often know they need to improve their foreign language ability but do not have the time to take a course. With intelligent use of computers, MP3 players, personal digital assistants (PDAs), and constantly improving high-speed Internet access, including wireless access, it will be possible to learn anywhere. Business correspondence and business reading in foreign languages will be easier and will contribute to constant learning. With the facilities for language learning which are now available, I think that in the future international business people will be naturally expected to communicate in more than one language.

Fish traps exist to capture fish.
Once you've got the fish you can forget the trap.
Rabbit snares exist to capture rabbits.
Once you've got the rabbit you can forget the snare.
Words exist to capture meaning.
Once you've got the meaning, you can forget the words.
Where can I find a man who has forgotten words?
I'd like to have a word with him!
– Zhuangzi, 4th century BC

THE ATTITUDE OF A LINGUIST

Just Communicate

Our ancestors created language in order to communicate. What a glorious invention! The ability to express our thoughts through language is what distinguishes us from animals. These great ancestors of ours did not have grammar or perfection in mind when they developed the first language, just the desire to get their meaning across. It may seem obvious, but to become a successful linguist you have to *want* to communicate in another language. People who are good at learning another language have a goal in mind, to communicate. That means to get to know people of another culture, not just to learn the rules of a new language as an academic subject. Unfortunately the emphasis on second language education in our school systems has caused many language learners to lose sight of this essential reason for language learning. In my own case, it was only when I became motivated to connect with a new culture and people that I was on my way to becoming a linguist.

Not all people are interested in meeting people of another culture and language. My wife Carmen and I were recently on holiday in California. When swimming in the hotel pool we heard the unmistakable sounds of people speaking Canadian English. There were two couples from Ottawa staying at the same resort. We joined them for a drink that evening. Interestingly both the wives spoke French and Spanish as well as English, but one of the husbands, an apparently successful businessman, was adamant that learning to speak languages was unnecessary. To him the important thing was to have good ideas. "You can always find a translator," he maintained.

I argued with him that human achievement, including business success, depended on communication. No matter how brilliant an idea, it needs to be communicated effectively in order to influence people. Surveys of employers consistently show the ability to communicate to be the most sought after characteristic in new employees. But, remembering Zhuangzi, I did not try too hard to enlighten this man. Obviously, learning languages was not in his nature.

Not all language learners are motivated to use the language they are learning. I remember clearly one day forty years ago when I was in charge of a language lab at the Agricultural Institute in Paris. One of my students suddenly groaned "*Merde*, I have been studying English for ten years and I still do not understand a thing!" With that, he flung down his headset and stomped out of the room. I can still see him.

I can sympathize with his frustration. He speaks for all the language learners who suffer through years of formal classroom language teaching, memorizing, drilling, answering questions, studying for tests– and yet do not achieve fluency. He was fed up with trying to learn words that were not relevant to him. He did not care about the content of what he was studying. He had no desire to communicate in English. The whole process was meaningless to him.

The natural linguist knows that to become fluent in a new language requires a commitment that goes beyond attending classes or studying textbooks. He or she knows that the new language must be discovered outside the classroom. A true linguist takes every opportunity to confront the new language in real life situations. Any learner who lacks this motivation to communicate in the new language is left struggling with the technical details of language and these are easily forgotten.

I remember how it was when I studied Latin in school. We had competitions to see who could decline Latin nouns the fastest, out loud. I could decline *bellum*, in both singular and plural, in a few seconds. It literally sounded like a blur. But I never had any intention of speaking Latin. I just wanted to pass tests. My high school French was similar. My Latin is now long since forgotten and I was unable to speak French properly until after I left high school.

In the quotation that starts this chapter, Zhuangzi tells us that even the very words of language are artificial creations. It is the heart to heart communication of meaning that is the essential nature of language, and therefore of language learning. All the rest is artificial. Fish traps are only useful for catching fish. Words are only useful if communication takes place. The learner has to *want* to start communicating.

Resistance to Language Learning

Even though I am an enthusiastic language learner, I am aware that not everyone wants to communicate in another language or learn about other cultures. It is understandable that many people are happier just using their own language and resist learning a new one. What is unfortunate, however, is that very often people who are trying to learn a second language are also actively resisting it.

Meeting a different language and culture can be stressful. It is certainly true that expressing thoughts and feelings in a new language is an intimate activity. Your language reflects your attitudes and personality, and therefore you feel most comfortable in your native language. It is also possible for people to resist a new language as a form of defense of their own language and identity. Some people feel inadequate and exposed when speaking in a second language. Some learners actually resent having to speak a new language, while others just find it tiring. People who are used to being able to freely and effectively express themselves in their own language are frustrated at the inability to put their ideas across in a second language.

This frustration can show in various ways. People all too often compare the new language to their own, rather than just imitating it and learning it. "Why does the new language say things this way? My native language is so much more logical, or elegant, or profound," they will often say. But these feelings simply betray their lack of familiarity with the new language. They are unwilling to relax and enjoy the experience of communicating in a new language and so they resist it.

These reactions are similar to how people may behave when they travel abroad. Whereas eager travelers simply immerse themselves in their destination and enjoy themselves, others are looking for reasons to say that, "after all, things are better at home." Either it is the food, or the cleanliness, or the weather that confirms to them that they were better off at home. Of course, we are always happy to come home from a trip, but why think of it while traveling? Speaking your native language *is* easier and more relaxing, but why focus on that while trying to communicate in a new language?

It is disappointing to see that many learners do not take advantage of the environments that surround them. It was true of me when I was growing up in Montreal. I found the same when I studied Political Science at the University of Grenoble, France in the early 1960s. There were many students from England and the United States who were there to study the French language. They were mostly interested in having a good time with other English speaking friends. They did not take full advantage of the opportunity of living in France. They were not sufficiently motivated to get to know French people. As a result, they did not improve their French as much as they could have.

In a similar vein, I once spoke with a Japanese professor of chemistry at a prestigious British university. He told me that, unfortunately, many of the language students from Japan at his university stay within their own language group. It was a common joke that students from Tokyo returned to Japan with an Osaka accent but little improvement in their English.

When we first learn to swim, the water can look uninviting. Until we commit ourselves, communicating in a foreign language can be the same. I remember hearing a recent immigrant to Canada tell me that after leaving his homeland, he first lived in Europe. He was invited to go out drinking with his co-workers but felt that he did not understand their sense of humor, so he stopped going out with them. He related this incident to me, quite out of context, presumably to convince me or himself that the cultural gap between him and "the foreigners" was simply too wide to bridge. Yet he wanted to improve his English. He did not realize that he had to learn to find common ground with "the foreigners" if he hoped to speak other languages fluently. He did not have the attitude of a linguist.

It is always easier to stay within your own cultural and linguistic group. I often hear recent immigrants to Vancouver tell me that they really like Vancouver. They can shop in their language, all the information they need is available in their language, there is radio, television and newspapers in their language and so forth. The only disadvantage to Vancouver is that they have a poor job because they cannot speak English very well. Now whose fault is that?

The personal, professional and cultural opportunities that come from being able to communicate in other languages are obvious. I derive enormous pleasure from speaking other languages, whether I am at home or traveling. What's more, I have built up my business through my ability to speak languages. Now, even when I am at home in Vancouver, it is not unusual for me to speak French on the telephone in the morning with a customer in Le Havre, or Swedish or German with suppliers, then chat with waiters over dim sum lunch in Cantonese, and then be on the telephone to Beijing or Nagoya in the evening speaking Mandarin and Japanese. I ran companies in Japan for six years. I have had occasion to give speeches to forest industry gatherings in Asia, Europe, Latin America and North America in Japanese, Spanish, Italian, French, and Swedish, as well as English.

Overcoming Resistance to Language Learning

To become a linguist you must overcome the different forms of resistance to the new language. It may take a personal relationship or sudden positive experience to break down this mental block to learning a new culture.

I remember an incident in Japan twenty years ago. I was selling lumber for a major Canadian exporter. We were having trouble getting our sawmills to produce the quality that the Japanese customers wanted. We arranged for our senior quality supervisor to come to Japan in order to better understand the customers' needs.

The first days were a disaster. Our man was from a small town in Canada and had worked at lumber grading and quality for his whole life. He had definite views on how lumber should be graded, and believed that it was not a matter of adjusting our sawmills' standards to the needs of the customers, but of showing the customers why they were wrong! In other words, our senior grader had a closed mind when it came to understanding the views of our customers.

One evening we went out on the town for a few drinks. We went to one of the bars in Japan where young ladies provide entertainment in the form of flattery and idle chit-chat. One pretty hostess asked our senior grader if he spoke Japanese. He gave her an intense star-struck gaze and answered, "No, but I can learn." He had a delightful evening at that bar.

From the next day, he started to see the Japanese customers' point of view and we were able to develop a new and successful Japanese lumber grade. This is the kind of event that should happen to every learner in order to soften resistance and increase interest in a language. The best opportunity to break down resistance to a new language is to make a friend in that language.

There are others who want to learn a new language and do not resist the new language , yetthey do not become linguists. They have another problem. They are afraid to make mistakes. These people put pressure on themselves to achieve accuracy or perfection at a stage when they have no feel for the language, and cannot visualize themselves comfortably using it. This is counterproductive and inhibits their ability to communicate by making them self-conscious. If you are willing to communicate at your level, even imperfectly, you will start to gain the confidence and the motivation to improve. Pronunciation, grammar and vocabulary can then be learned naturally, when the time is right.

By communicating and making mistakes I was able to learn and improve. Roughly forty years ago, in a university class in France, I was making an oral presentation. When I wanted to say the word "responsible", I said it with an "i" as in English, instead of "responsable" with an "a" as in French. Every time I pronounced it wrong there was laughter in the room. Only later did I realize that people were laughing at my mispronunciation. But it did not bother me that people were laughing at me. I was totally involved in giving my presentation and in getting my meaning across. I ignored the reason for everyone's laughter until later. But their laughter helped me. Now I never make that mistake.

Try to free yourself from the desire to achieve perfection. Mostly this desire for perfection is a form of vanity. I have had several well-educated learners tell me that they disliked listening to themselves speak English because they do not like to hear their own accent. This is mere vanity. The more concerned they are about how they sound the more tense they become. Tension inhibits their ability to pronounce correctly. My father spoke English very well but maintained a strong Czech accent all his life. It never bothered him, nor anyone listening to him.

Seeking perfection can only hinder your progress. Instead, seek to communicate naturally and enjoy yourself. Your improvement will be constant although uneven. You must believe that you have the ability to communicate in the new language and that by following the correct method you will achieve your goals. Just as in sports, confidence is an important ingredient for success.

In a very useful book about golf, Robert J. Rotella deals not with the techniques of golfing, but with developing the necessary attitude. The book is called *Golf is Not a Game of Perfect*. In golf, trying to be perfect undermines your enjoyment and your confidence, and therefore leads to poor performance. The same is true, if not more so, in language learning. To improve in golf it is important to practice, but it is critical to get out and enjoy the game regardless of your score. It is pointless to spend the whole time on the practice range. The same is true of language learning. Work to improve, by all means! But enjoy yourself when you communicate successfully in the new language.

Speaking a new language is like a game, especially at first. To be a linguist you have to enjoy communicating in a new language for its own sake, regardless of your level. Do not spend your time in a vain attempt to master the language from grammar rules and word lists. You will not enjoy this tedious form of study, and it will not work.

Communicate at Your Level

How do you communicate when you are learning a new language? Speaking and writing, as well as listening and reading, are all forms of communication in the new language. The key is to communicate in a way that suits your interests and skill level. When speaking, stay within your limits. Do not use slang, idioms or complicated words. Try to limit the conversation to subjects you can handle. Every time you communicate in a new language, even a little, pat yourself on the back and enjoy it. This will build up your confidence.

Even at the earliest stages of learning a language, your objective has to be to communicate, not to learn the language as an academic subject. It does not matter how much you struggle or how many mistakes you make, you will progress faster by communicating than trying to master theory.

My wife Carmen is a good example of this principle. When we lived in Tokyo she had little time to study Japanese, but she communicated very comfortably with all the shopkeepers in our neighbourhood by learning the names of the vegetables and fish that she wanted to buy.

Years later, we entertained our friends and customers from France, the Guillemettes, by spending a week driving them around British Columbia. Bernard Guillemette and I sat in the front and Carmen and Bernard's wife, Monique, who spoke only French, sat in the back. Carmen's grammar was atrocious but for one week she and Monique had a lively and enjoyable conversation in French in the back seat. I am sure that Carmen would be put in a beginner's class for grammar but she communicates better in French than most English-Canadians who have studied French at school for years. If she needs to improve her grammar she can do so, but at least she now has a sense for the language and some degree of confidence in communicating.

Carmen does not need to achieve fluency in French since she has only the occasional need to speak it. To use a language effectively in working situations requires real fluency, but for social purposes the ability to communicate is sufficient. Carmen has enough experience and confidence in casual communication that she could certainly achieve greater accuracy if she chose to pursue that as a goal.

It is the same when you listen and read: focus on subjects that are of interest or relevant to you. Your studies will be much more enjoyable and effective if you read or listen to aspects of the new culture that attract you or subjects that you need to learn about. Seeking out meaningful content is your first step to becoming a linguist. This can be on daily life, business, an academic subject that you know already, a hobby or common interest with a new friend, food, music, or whatever. You must articulate your reason for communicating. If you are only motivated by a sense of obligation to learn the language, you will just see a bunch of rules and words and language learning will be a difficult struggle.

The term "meaningful content" appears often in this book. It refers to real language situations, such as a conversation for a genuine purpose, rather than a dialogue in class or a drill or test question. It refers to reading and listening to content that is of interest and comprehensible to you. The more the context of your learning is realistic, the better you will learn. You will get beyond the details of the language you are learning and absorb the language naturally, because you are interested in the content. That is real communication. You will find what you are learning to be useful and therefore it will be easier to remember and retain.

Try to expose yourself to situations where you need the language. Many of the immigrants I mentioned earlier live their lives in their native language and then go to an artificial English environment in a classroom to try to improve their English. They would be better off to not attend class at all but try to do everything meaningful in their lives in English, such as shopping, banking, meeting with their children's teachers, etc.

I attended the 2001 Christmas Party of the Tsinghua University Alumnus Association of Vancouver. Tsinghua is the MIT of China, a world-class institute of engineering and technology. Graduates of Tsinghua who have immigrated to Canada have had varying degrees of success integrating into Canadian society. Often, graduates have difficulty finding work when they first arrive.

Two of the alumni I met at the party, who were the most fluent in English, had taken unusual approaches to plunging into Canadian society. One spent the first four months selling door to door in Surrey and Delta, communities where there are very few Chinese people. He had since moved on to a better job— but his English, after only four years in Canada, was outstanding! Another alumnus had only been in Canada one year but had opened a winemaking shop, which brought him into contact with the neighborhood. Rather than worry about their limited English or their status as highly educated professionals, these two people just plunged into a real context and as a result learned the language quickly.

These two successful learners were not vain or self-conscious about their English. They met people in a new language and communicated successfully. From that success they obtained the confidence which enabled them to improve their English. Learning a new language can be intimidating, especially for the first foreign language. However, by proceeding gradually and gaining small victories, your confidence will grow. It is important to remember that in learning a language you are not learning knowledge so much as acquiring a skill that takes time to develop. You have to get used to it. You are learning by *becoming*, not from theory.

You will not always perform equally well. When you play sports you are better on some occasions than on others, regardless of how much you practice. Language learning is the same way. Enjoy the moments when you are doing well and learn to forget the occasions when it seems that you are losing ground.

Once you have learned a second language, you will have the confidence to learn another one. In fact, the more languages you know, the better you will speak them all. You will even speak your native language better, because your ability to speak and to understand the nuances of meaning is enhanced when you learn new languages. You will be on your way to becoming a linguist.

Discover Language Naturally

We Englishmen, being far northerly, do not open our mouths
in the cold air wide enough to grace a southern tongue.
– John Milton (1644), English Poet

Each new language is a wonder of nature that we are all capable of discovering. The teacher can only stimulate, inspire and guide. It is up to you, the learner, to explore the language and absorb it gradually on your own terms. You should have the confidence that it is a natural thing for you to do.

Milton was wrong when he suggested that his northern countrymen were physically unable to learn southern languages. I have met many Englishmen who are excellent speakers of Italian and French. Milton undoubtedly knew that the even more northerly Vikings who invaded France in the 9th century had no trouble learning French in a generation. This was the language they spoke when, as Normans, they invaded England in the 11th century and proceeded to have a major influence in the development of the English language. Throughout history people have learned the language of other peoples quite naturally.

Today there are unprecedented opportunities to use foreign languages. There are many potential linguists throughout the world, people who want to communicate in another language. But too many of them tell themselves that is too difficult. Faced with complex grammar rules and dull textbooks, they give up. Seeing language learning as an extraordinary task can be a self-fulfilling vision, preventing you from achieving your potential. If you do not believe you can speak another language, you will certainly not succeed in doing so. You have to believe you can learn in order to achieve success. Accept the fact that you were born with the ability to learn to speak a new language, to be a linguist. You just have to find the way to develop this ability as an adult. You have to find a natural and enjoyable way of learning that suits your own personality, interests and available time.

We generally accept that everyone has an equal gift for learning their first language. Why should we assume that we require a special "gift" to learn a second language? Some people even claim that an ear for music is essential to language learning. A good place to test this theory is at a karaoke bar, where it can be easily demonstrated that there is no correlation between singing ability and language skills. We can all learn if we have the right attitude and if we find the method that is most suited to our nature.

I remember one evening in France, in a cafe with lots of international students, there was one student from Japan. He was a deaf-mute. Yet he was engaged in conversation with students from different countries by writing in his notebook. He wrote freely in thirteen languages. The determination and commitment of this individual was inspiring. One can only imagine the joy that his skill brought him. Although unable to hear or speak any language, he could communicate in thirteen! The more he communicated, the more he learned and improved. I am sure that he enjoyed learning a new language as much as practicing those that he already knew.

Some people may have better language learning ability than others, but this innate learning ability is not the decisive difference in language learning success. Why are so many Dutch or Swedish people good at learning languages, while Germans and English, not to mention Americans, are generally not as good at it? Why are French Canadians in general more successful in learning English than French people from France? Why are Chinese people from Singapore usually better at English than Chinese people from China or even from Hong Kong?

I do not believe that some nationalities have a better innate ability to learn languages than others. It is more likely that the big difference is attitude. The successful foreign language speakers take for granted that they will have to communicate in another language, and do not feel that it is an unusual thing to do. It is just expected. It is natural to them. Many Dutch or Swedish people realize that they need to speak foreign languages because few foreigners are going to learn Dutch or Swedish. Similarly, a large number of Singaporeans and Quebecois know they need English, and simply accept that they are going to be English speakers. There is no resistance. These people can all visualize themselves as fluent speakers of English.

I have met people of all nationalities who were comfortable speaking a foreign language. As a student in France, some of my close friends were, at different times, Turkish, Nigerian, Japanese, and Yugoslav. Yet we all communicated in French as if it were our language. We were not aware of our different nationalities. In retrospect, we were confirming the truth of Zhuangzi's comments. When we communicated naturally we were not aware of the words we were using.

The Limits of Language Teaching

Perhaps it is universal public education that has conditioned people to believe that learning can only take place in schools or in the classroom. Our school experience makes us think that learning is a passive activity. The student's task is to show up at school. The teacher's task is to impart knowledge. This is not the only way, nor even the best way, to learn languages.

Language needs to be discovered by the learner. Becoming a linguist depends on you, not on schools or teachers. Language teachers are dedicated to helping you improve, but they cannot make you fluent. You have to acquire the language yourself. The teacher can stimulate, explain, and provide the best possible language resources. After that, you must take charge and pursue your own learning, according to your own interests and nature. If you do that you will learn naturally and without stress.

The language classroom is too often an artificial environment where the emphasis is on *teaching* the language according to a timetable imposed by the curriculum. The expectation is that the teacher will deliver language knowledge or skills in a certain order. As long as the textbook is covered in the prescribed time period and test scores are positive, the assumption is that the language has been learned. Unfortunately, the results in terms of fluency are mostly disappointing.

The language classroom can be stressful. The learners often dislike having the teacher correct them in front of others, and are frequently frustrated at their own inability to speak properly. There is an underlying expectation that the students should perform correctly, rather than just communicate. The students alternately feel threatened or annoyed by their fellow students, depending on whether their classmates are more or less proficient at learning the new language than they are themselves.

I am not sure if this is the fault of the teachers or the learners. As someone who is motivated to learn languages, I am always surprised to see the passive attitude of so many language learners who willingly accept the obligation to show up for class but do not take initiative in their studies. If all students were genuinely motivated, and studied on their own, even conventional classes would be better learning environments. But maybe that is because our language teaching systems ignore the natural instincts and interests of the learner. If we allowed them to gradually perfect their skills following their natural inclinations perhaps they would work with more enthusiasm.

Potentially the greatest advantage of a classroom is the presence in one room of people who want to communicate in a language. In an ideal situation it would not be the language that is studied, but other subjects of interest to the students. In their desire to communicate naturally, the learners would absorb the language, and would be less self-conscious about their own language difficulties. They would not be interrupted with constant corrections. Rather, corrections would be provided at the end of the class in the form of suggested useful words and phrases to be learned.

I say this fully realizing that many language students claim that they want to be corrected by the teacher. But correcting mistakes is disruptive to the individual student and to other members of the class. A more natural and enjoyable use of the classroom is available by combining classroom teaching with effective e-learning.

Using the Internet it is possible for learners to select from a wide range of interesting language input for listening and reading. They can also learn words and phrases on their own using e-learning technology. Personalized coaching and writing correction services can also be provided via the Internet so that the student can come to class ready to engage in stimulating conversation.

The spread of small portable listening devices, hand-held computers, and wireless high-speed internet access will make it possible for learners to truly follow their interests and inclinations rather than having to conform to inflexible text books. Learners will be able to learn at their own speed, in a way suited to their needs, and at a time and place that is convenient. This seamless learning in small, customized doses will not do away with the classroom, but will change its role. The result should be to liberate potential linguists from the unnatural constraints of the classroom, and turn the classroom into a place to exchange ideas.

Another artificial obstacle to natural language learning is the frequent use of tests to evaluate learners. For a variety of reasons, educational authorities find it necessary to try to objectively assess the language competence of non-native speakers. For English, there are standardized tests which go by names like *TOEFL (Test of English as a Foreign Language)* and *TOEIC (Test of English for International Communication)* and similar acronyms. Many professors at universities and colleges in Canada have told me of their frustration over the number of foreign students who are able to enter university based on their TOEFL results, but in fact are unable to follow lectures and to write properly in English.

Some form of measurement of skills is necessary for university entrance, or for job interviews, but the standardized tests used are clearly not a reliable indicator of language fluency. I recognize that today they are a necessary evil but they should not become an obsession, and must never become the goal of language learning. There are other more accurate ways to measure the natural development of language skills without the stress of high-pressure tests like TOEFL. These new measurement tools can be used constantly to monitor progress and to identify areas of weakness.

Such constant feedback is helpful, but the best judge of your language competence is you, the learner. You know if you can read more easily, if you can understand more of what you hear, or if you are having an easier time expressing yourself. You should work on improving your overall language skills. Paradoxically, you will score better on these tests by acquiring a balanced ability in the new language rather than by just studying to pass these tests.

Too many language learners focus on doing well on these tests rather than on learning how to communicate comfortably. In preparation for tests, especially for the major standard tests, students will study word lists which are isolated from any content. They will spend countless hours reviewing specialized books with grammar rules, lists of verbs, phrases, idioms and sample questions. They study the techniques for getting high scores on these tests. In this way, they pursue study methods that are inefficient and stressful. In the long run, an undue emphasis on getting a high TOEFL or TOEIC score can divert you from the real goal of achieving fluency in the language. The test is only an interim goal on your way to academic and professional success. If you focus on test results without really learning the language, you are only fooling yourself. In the end, you will not be able to use the language effectively.

There are no shortcuts. To be comfortable in answering most TOEFL and TOEIC questions, you need to become familiar with the natural flow of the language in many different contexts. This can best be acquired through intensive listening and reading of a wide variety of interesting material while using a program that helps you remember new words and especially the most common phrases. This kind of exposure to the new language in real situations, not studying grammar and word lists, is the fastest and most enjoyable way to learn.

In some countries, especially in East Asia, fierce competition exists for entry into prestigious schools and universities. Foreign language ability is an important subject and school children are put through high pressure study programs to achieve good marks on national tests. There are cram schools with classes of fifty to seventy people. It is impossible to learn to communicate in these situations. Teachers devote themselves to revealing how to get high marks in this examination hell. I can well understand that this kind of teaching will discourage a learner's interest in a new language.

Public school systems everywhere have been widely unsuccessful in teaching second languages. This has had a negative influence on language learning. Many potential linguists are conditioned to think that language is a tedious subject that has to be taught in schools.

Given the importance of English for university entrance in many countries, it is surprising that more students do not choose a more natural way of learning, one that is more enjoyable and more effective. In fact, I believe the secret to successful natural language learning is closely related to the Taoist principles of effortlessness and pursuing one's own nature and interests. You need to train yourself and be aware of your own needs rather than just accepting constraints placed by others.

In my own case, I found studying theoretical explanations of grammar uninteresting and not an effective way to learn languages. I resisted doing exercises and answering questions that tested my knowledge of grammar. After I left high school, I discovered that I learned faster through systematic exposure to the language than if I relied on formal teaching in a classroom environment. Sentence structures that were strange and difficult at first eventually felt natural if I encountered them often enough in my reading and listening.

Occasionally I would consult grammar books to answer questions that I had about the language. Sometimes the explanations helped and at other times they did not. Much like when I looked words up in a dictionary, I would usually remember grammar rules or explanations (if I understood them) only for a short period of time and then forget them. In the end it was only through enough exposure to the language that my grammar improved.

Rather than trying to understand rules of grammar, the natural way to learn is to focus on systematic vocabulary acquisition based on lots of reading and listening to subjects of interest. You need to have initiative and curiosity. Teachers often complain that most of their learners lack this. However, if learners are allowed to learn from interesting content of their choosing rather than from artificial content, grammar rules and word lists, I believe many more will become self-directed learners.

I call the systematic pursuit of language using the three activities of listening, reading and learning words and phrases, the "engine" of language learning and describe it in more detail below. I believe most people can make language study more enjoyable, more creative and more productive by using this method. Unfortunately, too few learners choose this route. In fact, the "engine" approach to language learning is also a powerful way for native speakers of a language to increase their vocabulary.

I have had learners admit to me that the structured method of instruction that they experienced in their schooling was not effective. Yet they are prisoners of the system that failed them. These learners, whose English is neither natural nor fluent, still want to debate meaningless points of grammar. One student wrote an essay of 500 words for me to correct. There was a mistake every 10 words, mostly caused by a lack of familiarity with vocabulary. But rather than working on learning the appropriate phrases, this learner was mostly interested to try to justify her choice of a certain word based on grammatical arguments that I had difficulty following.

OCKHAM'S RAZOR

During the two years spent developing The Linguist language learning system, I visited bookstores and libraries in Canada, England, France, Germany, Japan, China and Sweden. I discovered a vast bibliography on many different aspects of linguistics, language teaching and grammar. As a person who has learned nine languages, I found the variety and complexity of this material astounding. I cannot say that most of this literature is wrong, but I found much of it not useful for language learning. I do not think that Zhuangzi would have approved. But then, as a Taoist he probably felt all science was futile.

In a recent short history of science entitled Universe on a T-Shirt (Penguin Canada), the Canadian science writer Dan Falk points out the importance of simplicity in scientific discovery. When competing explanations of natural phenomena are considered, it is almost always the simplest one, with the fewest assumptions, that is correct. This concept apparently is known to the science world as Ockham's Razor, in honour of William of Ockham, a monk who taught at Oxford and Paris in the 14th century and who first enunciated this principle. Ockham's Razor is most relevant to language learning where I think the basic principles are quite simple.

Constant exposure to interesting language content, if sustained for a long enough period of time, will bring success. Even learners at The Linguist sometimes forget this. One of our better learners was using The Linguist system regularly for English and was making good progress. Then she decided to stop using it to devote two months to preparing for TOEFL, practicing writing TOEFL tests and doing whatever one does to prepare for TOEFL. She did not pass TOEFL, but what was worse, her English ability stopped progressing, and in fact went backwards. To continue to progress in language learning you just need to practice the "engine"; listen, read, and learn words and phrases every day. It is that simple. Do this and speak when you have the chance. Try to write once a week. You will acquire the language faster this way than by all other ingenious tests, games or drills.

Another one of our regular learners, who was making good progress using our method, wanted to find a good grammar book. I told her that there were lots of good grammar books in the stores and that she should buy one as a reference. She replied that she was looking for a simpler grammar book that she could understand. I told her that if she learned enough phrases and if they became natural to her, then the grammar explanations would start to make sense. But first she had to learn the phrases.

There are no shortcuts to fluency. You need lots of exposure to the language. If you are not living where the language is spoken you need to work the "engine". Rules, word lists or specially prepared texts will not help you unless you are interested in the content. You will have trouble remembering specialized terms when you really need to use them. Instead, concentrate on learning the language from content that matters to you and interests you. Listen, read and learn the words and phrases. You will soon be able to deal with any language situation that may arise. That is the Ockham's Razor of language learning.

I was prepared to devote considerable effort away from class to listening and reading on subjects of interest to me. This was the natural and enjoyable way to discover the language. I developed my own systems for expanding my usable vocabulary, to ensure that I was able to retain words and phrases rather than immediately forget them if I did not see them again for a few days. I knew that my progress depended largely on my own efforts, and I was constantly motivated to find new content rather than rely on what was given to me in class.

There are undoubtedly learners who are happiest in the structured environment of a conventional language classroom and who prefer studying grammar and preparing for tests. Even those learners can benefit from becoming more self-directed in their learning. By customizing the learning process to suit their needs and interests, learners will find that even their classroom language experience will be more effective. In this way they will also make it possible to continue progressing in the language after the formal classes are ended.

Natural Learning

Speaking a new language is natural. You need only cultivate the latent capabilities that you already possess, but which need to be properly stimulated. As Steven Pinker points out in The Blank Slate (Penguin 2002), we have a natural intuitive capability to understand language. Therefore, languages can be learned in a natural manner, and an inherently interesting and pleasant manner. This is not the case for other subjects like modern science or mathematics, which require a more structured teaching approach, since we do not have the same intuitive ability to understand them.

The way of the linguist is one that leaves you free to pursue your own needs and interests, rather than having to learn according to an externally imposed program. You develop skills that you have within you. You integrate with the target language, listening and imitating rather than learning from theory.

When I was a child, and long before I had ever heard of Zhuangzi, I had a "Taoist" experience. My father could wiggle his ears. I could not. I wanted to learn how to wiggle my ears. I simply spent hours trying to will my ears to move. And eventually they did. My father did not teach me. He inspired me. We have the language ability within us. It is up to use to bring it out. Maybe we need to be more like children.

Man is most nearly himself when he achieves the seriousness of a child at play.
– Heraclitus

Children learn languages using natural methods. They just want to communicate. They cannot read grammar. They do not do drills. They do not prepare for tests. They just naturally want to learn. At birth, children of all nationalities have the same innate ability to learn a new language. It is true that children normally learn their mother tongue, but they possess a universal language instinct that will enable them to learn any language.

Children are exposed to a limited range of content which matters to them: the language of their parents and their friends at play. They concentrate on the words and phrases that are important to them and find opportunities to use them. They are not concerned about making mistakes of pronunciation or grammar. Children absorb the language without resistance. Unlike the classroom language learner, they are not constantly corrected but are encouraged in their efforts to speak. Unlike adults, they are flexible and uninhibited. Unlike adults whose first language constrains them, creating resistance, the child is free to absorb the language.

Children learn naturally, but adults can learn faster than children. It is always disappointing to hear adults say that they are too old to learn. They have a lifetime of experience and knowledge that can help them learn faster than any child. They are aware of concepts and phenomena that the child has not yet encountered. If adults can combine the curious and uninhibited learning attitude of the child with their own advantages, they can learn rapidly.

When I studied Mandarin Chinese or Japanese, I was able to read the newspaper and have serious discussions within six months. It takes a child much longer to reach that level of vocabulary. Adults can use their greater knowledge and broader interests to direct their learning, and can progress quickly.

As an adult language learner, you have a chance to create your own customized curriculum based on your interests. You can concentrate your learning on content that matters to you. It is only natural that you will remember words that are important to you but easily forget words that you feel are not useful. If you control your learning, you will learn faster. In listening and reading, comprehension depends on context. When listening to or reading material that you have chosen and where the background is familiar, your comprehension is higher than when you are struggling through uninteresting material. This is the natural way to build confidence and fluency in a non-stressful way.

Gradually your range of interests will take you into new areas, thus expanding your language ability. But the decision of what to study should be yours. Furthermore, if you accept the responsibility to seek out your own content, you will take a major step towards cultivating the self-reliant attitude needed for success in language learning.

Fred Genesee of McGill University, a leading researcher on language learning and the brain, explains what happens when we learn a new language:

When learning occurs, neuro-chemical communication between neurons is facilitated, in other words a neural network is gradually established. Exposure to unfamiliar speech sounds is initially registered by the brain as undifferentiated neural activity. As exposure continues, the listener (and the brain) learns to differentiate among different sounds and even among short sequences of sounds that correspond to words or parts of words...

Students' vocabulary acquisition can be enhanced when it is embedded in real-world complex contexts that are familiar to them.

Through intensive and repetitive exposure to enjoyable language material you will bathe your mind in the new language. This process is sometimes referred to as an "input flood" which trains your mind and prepares it for the more difficult task of expressing yourself in the new language. The linguist accepts the new language without resistance, confident that with enough exposure the difficulties of the language will gradually be overcome.

Language learning is not primarily an intellectual activity. It requires enthusiasm and repeated and concentrated exposure to language contexts that become familiar over time. I have often observed that foreign professional athletes in North America are good language learners, often more successful than foreign university professors. Hockey or basketball players are able to deliver fluent interviews on television, whereas the more intellectual professors are likely to have very strong accents and speak in a more stilted and unnatural manner. The reason is that athletes have constant informal verbal interaction with teammates. They need to fit into the team or they will not perform well. They learn quickly, immersed in the comfortable and familiar environment of their sport.

Unlike the athlete on a team, most language learners are not exposed to constant and familiar language contexts. That is why it is so important to create your own curriculum based on learning contexts which cater to your interests and needs. Following your interests is the natural way to learn. The greater your range of interests, the more curious you are about the world around you, the better you will learn.

Identity and Language

Languages are unlike any other subject taught in a classroom in that they involve the acquisition of skills and behaviour patterns which are characteristic of another community.
– R.C.Gardner, Social Psychology and Language Learning, the Role of Attitudes and Motivation

With your first encounter with a foreign language you are coming into contact with an "other," another language and another culture. But actually that "other" is not as foreign as you think. In time the new language and culture can become natural to you, a part of who you are. You become a linguist when you accept the fact that you can change. You can acquire skills and behaviour patterns characteristic of another culture. I have done it many times, and have seen others with no previous experience of language learning do the same.

In his excellent book *El Bosque Originario* (Ediciones Taurus), on the genealogical myths of the people of Europe, the Basque philosopher Jon Juaristi writes:

There is no nation without its tale or tales of origin. These myths are based on the logic of exclusion, of a difference constructed on the basis of exalting Us and negating the Other. Recurring themes like aboriginality, divine selection, purity of blood or language are supports of different variants of a common narrative.

The linguist knows that the differences between people, exalted in such traditions, are not based on biology but on education. The linguist sees these differences but also sees similarity. The linguist is able to grow as a person and accept elements of a new culture as part of his or her larger human identity.

Charles Pasqua, the former French Minister of Immigration, once said that when an immigrant arrives in France, his ancestors become the Gauls, the ancient Celtic people who lived in France at the time of the Roman Empire.

The resonance of M. Pasqua's statement is not diminished by the fact that M. Pasqua, like new immigrants, had ancestors who were not Gauls. However, in French history and French myths of origin, the Gauls were important. Pasqua is French, so at least symbolically, his ancestors were the Gauls. This is part of his sense of belonging to the group.

In a similar sense, as a human being, I consider all ancient people as my ancestors. I can choose to partake in any of the traditions and cultures I see around me if I make the effort to learn them. As a result of having learned French I am able to participate in French culture and consider it a part of who I am. When I approached the study of Chinese, it was in order to make this previously unknown culture a part of me, to explore my human heritage. In learning new languages it is never my intention to compare different cultures to see which is "better," but to acquire something new and valuable and expand as a human being. As a linguist it is important to let go of the security of your native language and culture and broaden your identity.

Speaking a new language means imitating its native speakers, how they speak, and to some extent how they act. When I speak French, I try to become French; when I speak Chinese, I try to be Chinese; when I speak Japanese, I act as if I am Japanese. Largely this is a form of theatre and not a change of personality. But people do observe that my facial expressions and gestures change when I speak different languages.

As Steven Pinker points out in "The Blank Slate", we are not born with our culture but it is something we acquire by imitating. Culture is a set of behaviour patterns that are useful for survival in a given environment and which we learn from those around us. Faced with a different language environment, some people are able to adopt this new culture and others are not. Those that are become good language learners.

The less you are constrained by your first culture the easier you can imitate the second. People who speak one second language are usually better able to learn more languages because the constraints of their native language and its culture have been overcome. Remember that "imitation is the sincerest form of flattery." Seek out people that you like or enjoy listening to in the second language and imitate them. Of course, there is more to language learning than this. There are deliberate learning activities that are described in the next section. However, your eventual success or failure to effectively communicate in a new language will be largely determined by your willingness to step outside your native culture, at least in your imagination.

Until we become fluent in a new language, when we speak it we should engage in a certain degree of play-acting. Have fun and pretend that you are what you are not. You should empty your mind of your original culture for a while in order to better absorb the language you are learning. You do not give up your original identity, and that is certainly not the aim of language learning. But you do acquire the ability to understand the values and way of thinking of another culture.

I was a butterfly, flying contentedly
Then I awoke as Zhuangzi.
And now I don't know who I really am—
A butterfly who dreams he is Zhuangzi
Or Zhuangzi who dreamed he was a butterfly.
– Zhuangzi

Sports psychologists encourage competitive athletes to visualize their success. Paul Kariya is one of the top ice hockey players in the world. My younger son, Mark, played hockey for Yale University against Paul Kariya when Kariya played for Maine University. Apparently, Kariya sat for an hour before each game and visualized himself making plays against the players on the other team. Paul Kariya is a player of relatively small physical stature who has reached the highest world level in a game of strength and speed. I am sure this technique helped him. Be like Paul Kariya: visualize your success! Try to visualize yourself as a fluent native speaker.

Visualize yourself pronouncing like a native speaker and thinking in the language. The ability to reason in the logic of other languages exists within all of us. It is there for you to develop. In that sense, language learning is a process of self-discovery. You need to accept the spirit of the new language, even if it seems strange at first. Let it be a force for uncovering your latent language abilities. There is no need to fear losing the logic or values of your native language. You will only be enriched by acquiring additional languages and new perspectives.

We have the potential to penetrate other cultures regardless of our background, as long as we are curious enough to do so. There are many examples of people who were outstanding artists in a second culture. Joseph Conrad, a Pole, is a leading figure of modern English literature. Samuel Beckett, an Irishman, wrote one of the prominent plays of modern French literature, *Waiting for Godot*. There are many outstanding non-European virtuosos performing European classical music. Many non-Asians dedicate themselves with success to Asian arts or traditional sports.

The Fundamental Similarity of Human Beings

With the discovery of DNA, we now understand what the Taoists knew intuitively: all is one. Human beings are remarkably uniform and have a common origin. As Richard Dawkins brilliantly explains in *River Out of Eden*, our genes have been handed down to us by those of our ancestors who survived long enough to produce children. Many of our characteristics, such as blood type and susceptibility to certain diseases, cut across the lines of more superficial differences like skin colour or body shape. While we may look different from each other today, every person alive has a common male ancestor who lived around 50,000 years ago. To quote again from Spencer Wells in *The Journey of Man, A Genetic Odyssey*, "Physical traits that distinguish modern human geographic groups only appear in the fossil record within the past 30,000 years. Most older fossils of Africans, Asians and Europeans are very similar to each other."

Our genes are so common that they can cohabit with the genes of other human beings of any nation or race to create members of a next generation. Genetic differences between individuals are greater than the genetic differences between ethnic groups. And any one of us can speak any language.

I have been told that there are people who have paid money to have an operation on their tongues in order to be able to better pronounce a foreign language. Whether this is true or not, I cannot say, but the fact that such a story is told is an indication of the persistence of the association of language with ancestry. If you were adopted at birth by someone of a different race, you would naturally learn to speak their language without needing a tongue operation.

Human Culture is Universal

Just as with genes, human culture has passed from generation to generation, its form and content constantly evolving. Like the genetic makeup of people, human culture is universal despite its variations. The source of world culture is everywhere the same: human creativity. Twenty-five hundred years ago, philosophers in China, India and Greece dealt with the same human issues as we do now, and their thoughts are readily understood by people of many different cultures today.

In fact, a closer study of the thoughts of Heraclitus, Zhuangzi, and Buddha show remarkable similarities between them. Their philosophies are not just accessible to Greeks, Chinese or Indians. These thinkers have had an influence that greatly exceeded their time and country. The explanations that humans have sought to solve the riddles of human existence are universal. It is precisely this universality of human thought and feeling that makes learning foreign languages such a natural and rewarding adventure.

All cultures are connected. The ancient civilizations of the Middle East spawned a literary revolution that dramatically influenced the course of history. The Semitic alphabet, the mother of all alphabets, indirectly made possible Greek and Indian philosophical writings and the books of the great religions. As thoughts were written down, it became possible for others to read them, ponder them and comment on them. Chinese writing had the same effect on East Asian cultures. It is on these foundations that the modern world is built.

In more recent times, the development of European science and the industrial revolution were dependent on Chinese technology, Indian mathematics and Arabic cultural influence. Religions created in the Middle East and India dominate the world, while much of the world's popular music is influenced by African rhythms.

Our modern world is the result of an ongoing process of cultural creativity and interaction that started with the first humans. Migration, trade, conquest, cultural exchange, cultural synthesis and assimilation have been the constant pattern of history on all continents. Globalization is not a recent phenomenon; it is just that the speed and the scale have increased as modern communications have shrunk the globe.

Individuals in a Shrinking World

Canada is an interesting example of a country where cultures are mixing and a new identity is emerging. Perhaps Canada is at the same stage in its evolution as older societies in Europe or Asia were one thousand or several thousand years ago. Over the last fifty years, Canada has absorbed many different peoples who are today united through their common language, either English or French. The process of blending in can take time, but today a "native speaker" of Canadian English can be of African, East Asian, South Asian, Mediterranean, Northern European, First Nation or any other single or mixed origin.

Human beings feel closest to family and kin. Beyond the family, however, the nature of the "in group" can vary depending on circumstances. Anthony Smith, who directed my older son Eric's post-graduate study at the London School of Economics, wrote an important book entitled ***National Identity*** (Penguin). In it, Smith distinguishes two visions of national identity, which have been promoted by ruling and intellectual elites in modern times.

In one vision of national identity:

...nations must have a measure of common culture and a civic ideology, a set of common understandings and aspirations, sentiments and ideas, that bind the

population together in their homeland. The task of ensuring a common public, mass culture has been handed over to the agencies of popular socialization, notably the public system of education and the mass media.

In the other vision of national identity:

Whether you stayed in your community or emigrated to another, you remained ineluctably, organically, a member of the community of your birth and were forever stamped by it. A nation, in other words, was first and foremost a community of common descent....or rather presumed descent.

Canada is of the first kind. As the nature of human societies continues to evolve, I am convinced that attempts to freeze people's identity based on their ancestry will prove vain.

My own case is an example of the impermanent nature of national identity. My parents were born into a German speaking Jewish community in the Austro-Hungarian Empire in an area that subsequently became Czechoslovakia and then the Czech Republic. My parents moved to Sweden in 1939. I was born in 1945 in Sweden and my family moved to Montreal in 1951.

My national identity is Canadian, specifically English Canadian. However, depending on different historical factors beyond my control, I could just as easily have ended up Austrian, Czech, Swedish, Israeli, or a French speaking Quebecois. Despite accelerated globalization, national or regional identities are not disappearing, and in fact may be getting stronger. However, today we have more freedom to choose our identity.

We are all individual human beings. We can share in different identities and understand different cultures. We are stamped by our native culture but this is an accident of history. It cannot limit us. As individuals we have the opportunity and, I would say the responsibility, to explore other cultures. The best way to do that is through language.

The pupil is ... "schooled" to confuse teaching with learning, grade advancement with education, a diploma with competence.
- **Ivan Illich, Educator and author, Deschooling Society (1973)**

HOW TO LEARN A LANGUAGE

Conviviality

By now you understand that learning does not only take place in a school. Learning is done by individuals who want to acquire knowledge from others or from the world around them. My own success as a linguist has been driven by an interest in languages and the pursuit of conviviality in the sense that Cicero meant it - enjoying the company of others because they share our lives, regardless of their country or language.

This attitude of autonomy, combined with a desire for human communication, is common to many people around the world. The world is full of potential linguists who only need to find the best way to develop their abilities. Are you one of these people?

> The famous Austrian linguist and philosopher Ivan Illich proposed the creation of convivial learning webs as a substitute for the formal education system dominated by "experts." These convivial webs were to be informal communities which provided resources for independent-minded people to learn and share knowledge in a manner that was more effective than formal schooling. Illich's vision was ahead of its time but it gave a strong hint as to how language learning could be organized in the age of the Internet.

How can a convivial language learning environment work in practice? Today the Internet can offer a varied and constantly growing collection of language content; interviews with real people in different walks of life and in different languages, as well as texts on many subjects, both fiction and non-fiction. This content is available in audio and text format. The audio can be downloaded and the text can be read on the Internet. Online dictionaries and customized databases for words and phrases greatly assist in vocabulary learning. In addition, modern technology makes available pronunciation and writing correction systems which are effective and practical. The Linguist is just one system that takes advantage of these opportunities.

On the Internet, learners can create communities of members who can communicate with other learners and native speakers using instant messaging and email, voice-chat, video-chat or even face to face meetings. Members can organize different events, with or without native speaker coaches. In this convivial learning community, it is up to the learners to take the initiative and to discover the language themselves. In this way they learn faster and more enjoyably.

I am often asked by learners to recommend a specific plan of study for them. "What should I do every day?" "Which words should I learn?" they ask. My answer is a combination of Taoism and Japanese quality control.

You must rely on yourself and follow your interests. If you follow your interests you will be motivated. You must learn from the language as closely as you can, listening, observing and imitating. So much for the Taoist part. But you must measure what you do. Measure your input and measure your output to make sure you are on course to achieve your objective. That is the quality control part.

Input not grammar

As a language learner, you want to learn to express yourself comfortably in a new language. This is certainly achievable. Before you can express yourself, however, you need to absorb the new language. You can only absorb the language through massive input. You will not be able to use the language until you have acquired enough of it to be able to communicate meaningful thoughts. To acquire the language you must focus on input first, and continue this commitment to input for most of the period of your language study. Until you are fairly comfortable in the language, correct grammar should be a secondary consideration.

Language is best acquired by using what I call "the engine", a powerful synergy of three essential language learning activities; listening, reading, and the systematic study of words and phrases. The mechanics of the "engine" will be described in this chapter.

Listen

The first thing to do is to listen. My experience with learning Chinese, Japanese and other languages has confirmed to me that the best way to improve fluency and comprehension is the seemingly passive activity of listening over and over to understandable content. This activity allows you to expand your language skills in a non-stressful way. Listening is not just for beginners. I still listen to my favourite tapes in languages that I already speak well: in my car, while walking or jogging, or doing chores around the house. You can always improve pronunciation, rhythm, vocabulary and fluency.

Start by choosing content at your level and just listen. If you are a beginner, you may choose short items of a few lines. Later you will be able to handle content of two to five minutes in length. As you progress you will want to listen to content that is twenty minutes in length or even longer. Listen to the same content over and over. The subject should be of interest, the voices pleasing to you, and the level not too difficult. The more familiar the background, the easier it will be for you to understand.

Get in the habit of listening frequently: in the morning, during the day and in the evening. Make sure you get a convenient portable listening device such as a Minidisc recorder, MP3 player, or CD player. Take the trouble to learn how to download content and then record it onto your portable device. This way you do not have to buy CDs or tapes but can quickly download what you want. You don't need to sit in a room beside a tape recorder like I did when I was learning in the late 1960s. Nor should you just sit in front of your computer listening to content streamed at you. Do as I did when I learned Cantonese at the age of fifty-five. Download the content or buy CDs and take your lessons with you when shopping, driving, exercising, washing the dishes and cleaning the garage. That is how to accumulate the necessary exposure to the language.

When you first listen to new content, you need only get used to the sounds. Try to get a sense for the rhythm. Do not worry if you do not understand all of it. Listen a few times without reading the text. Then read the text carefully, look up new words in an online dictionary, and save new words and phrases to a list for later review.

Even after you basically understand a text, you need to listen, over and over, to make this content part of your subconscious. You may have to read the text again and you will certainly review the new words and phrases many times. But mostly you should listen.

Especially in the early stages, focus on a small amount of content and get used to it, rather than trying to listen to constantly changing content. By listening to the same content repeatedly, you will get better at hearing where one word or phrase ends and the next one begins. You will also start to recognize familiar words when you listen to new content. Let the phrases ring in your mind even after you stop listening. Repeat certain phrases out loud. Try to imitate the correct pronunciation.

Repetitive listening is like physical training. You are training your mind to process the new language. Short, frequent listening sessions can be better than fewer longer sessions. Try to listen for one hour a day, broken into short segments of ten to thirty minutes at a time.

I have never been in favour of modern audiovisual learning materials such as computer assisted interactive games or other tests and quizzes which create artificial learning environments. I did not enjoy being tested on my comprehension of what I was listening to. I resisted questions that forced me to try to remember what I had heard. I preferred to listen again, or to listen to new material, or to engage in a general conversation on the subject of my listening. I always felt that natural communication was a more effective way to learn.

Listening is real communication. When you are listening, you are absorbed in a pure language environment. You have to use the sounds of the language to imagine the meaning. Repetitive listening is an ideal learning environment, as long as you choose content of interest to you, content that you want to understand. You should build up an ever-expanding library of such material as part of a lifelong language learning strategy.

Make sure you listen attentively when speaking to native speakers. Do not be so concerned about what you are saying that you are not picking up the intonation and phrases used by native speakers. Every chance to hear the new language is an opportunity to learn and improve.

In December of 2003, I decided to take up Korean just to experience learning a new language from the beginning. I bought several language learning systems, which consisted of texts, grammar explanations and CD's. I ignored the grammar explanations, but used the vocabulary lists to work my way through the reading of the texts. Mostly, I just listened to the CD's. I found other Korean textbooks which I asked a Korean friend to record for me onto a MD player. I even found some Korean content on the Internet which consisted of texts and MP3 files. I downloaded the audio files and transferred them to onto my MP3 player. I was able to listen well over an hour every day by fitting in 10 to 30 minute periods of time throughout the day. I listened to easy material and more difficult material and then back to easy material and so on. My progress in Korean has been rapid.

But once past the beginner stage, I faced the frustration of every intermediate learner. How do I go forward to real fluency? I am tired of listening to dialogues between fictitious students at the library, at the restaurant, at the post office, at the hospital, at the train station and so on. I know how to say that the traffic in Seoul is very bad and that the subway is convenient. I have visited certain historic sites in Korea and have learned about King Sejon who invented the Korean script. Now I want real language situations on subjects of interest to me. I also need a way to use such authentic content to learn. As I will explain, modern computer technology makes it possible to do just that.

Reading

If listening is the first point in the "engine" of language learning, reading is the second. It is said that some people are visual learners and some people learn better by hearing. But all learners can benefit from doing both. Read and listen to the same content over and over to reinforce your learning. Doing both activities will train your mind in the new language

At first you need to read to understand what you are listening to. But even once you understand a text, reading it again will help create fluency and confidence. If you are regularly listening to the same text, the words and the sounds of the words can come alive as you read. This mutual reinforcement between reading and listening is made much more effective if the content is of interest to you.

As you progress in your learning, you will read to gain new vocabulary and to learn about the culture and other subjects in your new language. Wherever possible, seek out the audio version of what you are reading. If you have friends who are speakers of that language, ask them to record texts that you find interesting.

Reading, and reading a lot, is essential to achieving fluency in a new language. To read a lot you must make it enjoyable by finding material to read that is interesting. The Internet opens up a limitless source of interesting reading material, consisting of newspapers, magazines and many specialized articles, e-books and other material. Reading on the computer has many advantages. With the computer it is possible to use online dictionaries and other functions that make reading in the new language a powerful learning experience.

Reading should be a growing part of your learning activities. As your vocabulary and confidence increase, you will read more conventional print versions of books and periodicals in the new language. When reading away from the computer, you should ignore the few words you do not know and just enjoy yourself. I sometimes found it a struggle to read in a foreign language when there were so many words I did not understand. If I was interested enough in the content I would persevere. Gradually, my ability to read in a number of languages improved. I now read these languages for information and enjoyment rather than as a learning task. Whether you are a native speaker or a non-native speaker, reading widely will enhance your ability to express yourself clearly and eloquently.

Learning Words and Phrases

The third point in the language learning "engine" is the study of words and phrases. Listening and reading are sometimes referred to as "top-down" learning tacivities. When you study the words and phrases, you are engaged in "bottom-up" learning. You are focused on the components of the language. The systematic study of the components is a necessary element in the acquisition of language. The effective use of modern technology makes the study of words and phrases more effective than ever.

When I studied languages in the past, and even now for my study of Korean, I had to search bookstores for language readers with vocabulary lists in order to avoid the time consuming activity of using a conventional dictionary. But these vocabulary lists were not customized to my needs, and the content in these readers was often not interesting to me. Many of the words on the vocabulary list were known to me, whereas words that I did not understand were often not explained. There was no way for the editor of the book to predict what I knew and did not know. While reading, I would constantly refer to these vocabulary lists as a crutch, instead of developing the important ability to guess at the meaning of a word from the content around it. Using these word lists was a necessary evil. It enabled me to read new material but it also distracted me in my reading. Another problem with studying word lists is that, just as with looking up words in a dictionary, I forget words almost as quickly as I learn them.

You need a systematic way to expand vocabulary in order for the language acquisition "engine" to really work effectively. That is what I am missing in my Korean learning. That is what I need to really improve my knowledge of Chinese. The task is daunting. You need to learn more than 10,000 words and phrases to reach a university or professional level of fluency in a language like English. I have read that a seven year old knows 7,000 words in English and a 14 year old knows 14,000 words. A university graduate may know 50,000 words. How can a foreign learner acquire enough words to interact effectively at work or at university with the native speaker?

It has been established that in English the most frequent 1,000 words account for roughly 75% of most language content. The next 1,000 most frequent words account for only another 5%. Presumably the same is true in other languages. The remaining 20% of the words, that are not high-frequency words, are essential to the meaning. How can you acquire these words when they appear so infrequently? This is the challenge in vocabulary acquisition.

Fortunately you do not need to learn 50,000 words. You should make sure you fully master the most common 2,000 words and then specialize in areas of interest to you. Perhaps 10,000 words are sufficient for professional and academic purposes in North America, perhaps even less. A vocabulary of 6,000 words will probably allow you to do quite well on TOEFL. However TOEFL has proven to be an unreliable measure of language skills. Probably you need to learn more vocabulary than you realize.

Learning new words and phrases can be frustrating. New words are easy to forget and complex words and phrases can have subtle shades of meaning which vary depending on context. Vocabulary learning is often handled in an inefficient manner by learners. Learners look words up in a dictionary and then forget them. They write lists which they never refer to. They have no record of what they have learned, and what they still need to learn. Often learners study isolated lists of words and phrases in the hope that they will remember them for tests. There is a better way.

As you progress you will soon run out of texts with vocabulary lists. You need to deal with authentic content. You need to create your own lists of words and phrases. Just as you choose what to listen to and read, you should also decide which words and phrases from your listening and reading will be most useful to you. By choosing your own vocabulary items rather than being spoon-fed, you will remember them better.

For this to work you must take advantage of the benefits of electronic text. By reading on the computer you can obtain instant explanations and translations of new words from dictionary software programs. You can enter new words and phrases into a personal database, where they can be managed in many useful ways to enhance learning. You can create customized lists of these words and phrases, based on subject matter, function in the sentence, or root words. Such customized lists drawn from your listening and reading are far more useful than the "Word Books" and "Phrase Books" that are sold widely to language learners.

In this way the computer makes possible a systematic way of learning new words and phrases that greatly enhances the effectiveness of the language acquisition "engine". In addition, with the computer it is possible to introduce measurement. You can now measure not only the amount of time you are spending but also how many words you have learned and your progress towards your goals. Not only is this motivating, but it helps you to evaluate the difficulty of new texts, which can be compared to your known words.

Even with the enhanced learning effectiveness provided by the computer, there are no shortcuts. To expand your vocabulary you have to listen and read a great deal. You need to be systematically working to add to your knowledge of words and phrases You need to review them regularly. This is the engine of language learning.

Vocabulary consists of words and phrases. Words are easier to measure, but learning new phrases is now widely recognized as essential to learning to express yourself like a native speaker. These phrases can be any group of two or more words that are useful for you to express yourself. The phrases used by the native speaker are the basic components of the language. If you choose these phrases from texts that you are listening to and reading, these phrases will be more meaningful to you than phrases that are provided out of context. By choosing your own phrases and reviewing them regularly you will make these phrases a part of your daily language. As you become accustomed to using them, you not only acquire strings of new words, you also naturally acquire correct grammar.

Many learners want to be provided with lists of phrases to learn. This is not the most effective way to learn. To be able to use phrases you need to earn them. You need to discover them yourself from your reading and listening. You need to find them in their natural context.

The systematic learning of phrases is the most effective way to learn to express yourself accurately in a new language. I do not believe grammar should be taught using rules or tests. Grammar is an abstraction, a theoretical explanation of the function of words. Grammar represents a standard of good practice and can be a useful reference. There are many good grammar books around, and you should refer to them for specific help on problems you have encountered. Trying to memorize the rules of grammar, however, can be a distraction from learning the language. Grammatical explanations often introduce an artificial level of theory, with new technical terms that can be more confusing than helpful. Especially in the early stages, you should not let a concern about grammatical accuracy prevent you from communicating in the new language.

Focus your efforts on phrases as the essential building blocks of language. This will improve your structure and style. You will have an easier time understanding the spoken language and you will sound more like a native speaker if you have trained yourself in phrases. This emphasis on phrases starts with the first "How are you?", and continues right up to the most advanced stage.

To learn a language quickly you need to develop the habit of working different points in the language acquisition "engine" every day. Some days you will listen more, and some days you will read or study words and phrases more. This regular interaction of listening and reading with the study of specific components creates the synergy required to make a breakthrough in language acquisition. What is more, if this process is based on content of interest to you, you will find it enjoyable and satisfying in a way that traditional language learning is not. You will find that you will no longer need detailed study schedules nor ask for so many grammar explanations or ready made lists of words and phrases. But for this to work you must measure what you do.

The activities of the "engine" are also effective for native speakers of a language who wish to build up their vocabulary in their own language. A deliberate program of reading well-written books, when combined with listening to the audio version of these books and the systematic study of new words and phrases from these books can give native speakers a much richer vocabulary and the ability to express themselves in their own language. This can make the difference between success and mediocrity in many professions. How you speak your own language says a lot about who you are. It is a powerful expression of your identity. It can be more important than your physical appearance and the clothes you wear in influencing others and achieving your goals in life.

Learn To Express Yourself

As you acquire a new language using the "engine" method, you will start to feel the confidence to start talking with native speakers. As you do so, there will be times when you successfully express your thoughts on something that is important to you. You feel a sense of triumph. Unfortunately, this happy moment is often followed by another encounter where you find yourself tongue-tied and unable to really say what you want to say. Comfortable fluency takes time and practice. It is the ultimate goal and is certainly achievable for everyone. However, it need not be rushed.

To express yourself in a new language you must first absorb the language by listening, reading and learning vocabulary as explained above. These activities will always account for about three quarters of your effort while you are working to achieve a basic level of fluency. But from the beginning you also have to allocate some time to work on your skills of expression: pronunciation, writing and conversation.

Just as you measure your input "engine" activities, you should measure your output activities. You should measure not only the effort you put into output activities, but also the degree of language accuracy and richness that you are achieving. In this way you have a constant measure of your progress and an indication of where you need to make additional efforts.

Steve Kaufmann

Pronunciation

Pronunciation should be a major area of emphasis from the beginning, and throughout the first period of studying a new language. You should commit to spend a certain number of hours per week working on pronunciation, especially during the early stages of your studies. Many learners do not put enough deliberate effort into pronunciation and resign themselves to speaking as if they were pronouncing their native language.

Any person can learn to pronounce any language, regardless of nationality. Some people may achieve better results than others, but we can all get pretty close if we work at it. The objective should be to be easily understood. It is not necessary, nor possible for everyone, to achieve near native speaker pronunciation.

Mandarin Chinese, with its four tones, is very different from English. Nevertheless, I was determined to master Mandarin pronunciation, and to learn to speak like a native. I believe I have come pretty close, perhaps because I did not consider the possibility that I could not do so. In fact, I made pronunciation the major focus of my early effort, and I recommend this to you as well. It takes longer to get a feel for speaking in a grammatically correct manner, but you can work on pronunciation from the beginning.

In order to learn to pronounce correctly, you need to develop the ability to hear the sounds of the new language. This takes time. There are four key steps to developing pronunciation accuracy.

First, LISTEN repeatedly to individual sounds and to material within your basic range of comprehension, concentrating on pronunciation. Listen carefully to the intonation. Try to become conscious of the rhythm and breathing pattern. Try to identify separate words and phrases. With repetition, this gradually becomes easier. The language sounds strange at first but will become more familiar with repetitive listening.

Second, REPEAT individual words and phrases out loud, both during and after listening. You will remember certain phrases. Try to say them over and over again to yourself while doing other tasks. You will have trouble with certain sounds. Work especially hard to master them. Then practice repeating phrases and sentences with the proper emphasis and intonation.

Third, READ sentences and paragraphs out loud, first very slowly and then more quickly, and always in a loud voice. Imagine you are a native speaker. Exaggerate - pretend you are an actor. Have fun with it! You should alternate between reading unfamiliar material, and reading something that you have written and had corrected.

Fourth, RECORD your own pronunciation and compare it to a native speaker. This will train you to hear the differences in pronunciation between yourself and a native speaker. You have to hear it to be able to pronounce it! Recording your own pronunciation also serves as a record of your progress as your pronunciation improves.

The sounds, the intonation and even the writing system of your native language can influence your pronunciation of the second language. The more you are able to establish freedom from the influence of your native language, including the influence on pronunciation, the better you will learn the second language. The writing and sound system of the native language can be significant obstacles for a learner since there is a natural tendency to pronounce the words of a new language as if they were a word in your own language.

In Japanese the writing system is based on syllables. So a word like "brother" becomes "bu-ra-za." In Korean there is no "f" sound. Many North Americans seem unable to pronounce the Japanese Kato or Sato to rhyme with "sat" and "cat" even though those words exist in English. They may hear these names pronounced correctly many times, but still insist on pronouncing their names to rhyme with "say" or "gay". Cantonese pronounce from the throat, Mandarin speakers speak more with the tip of their tongue, and people from central China do not distinguish between "l" and "n". The Spanish pronounce "w" as "gu" and the Germans pronounce "w" as "v," the Swedes say "yust" instead of "just," the French cannot pronounce "h" and on it goes.

It is important to practice pronunciation while reading the new language to get used to seeing these words as words in that language. You have to force yourself to train the muscles of your mouth to make the new sounds accurately. You may have to breathe differently to pronounce the new language correctly. You must try to imitate the rhythm of the new language. Pronunciation practice is best done on your own, and is a form of play-acting. It can be fun.

Learn to be your own toughest pronunciation critic when you are working on it alone, and then forget about it and be relaxed when speaking to others. People are unlikely to comment on your pronunciation, as long as you are easily understood. Remember that perfection is not the goal, just comfortable communication. If you cannot completely imitate native pronunciation do not worry, as long as you can comfortably make yourself understood. I know many people who express themselves very elegantly in English, probably better than most native speakers, and yet still have an accent. This is not a problem.

Often, learning proper "body language" can be as important as pronunciation in effective communication. Easily understanding what is said is essential to good body language. Furthermore, an appreciation for the culture of the language you are speaking is more important than good pronunciation. If you are genuinely interested in communication, and not just in the vanity of perfection, your pronunciation will quickly cease to be a problem. I know non-native speakers who have almost native-like pronunciation but do not understand the language as well as others who speak with strong accents. As with all aspects of language learning, it is the ability to communicate effectively that has to be the most important goal.

Writing

The ability to write clearly is required for entrance to university and for many workplace situations. Some learners may not feel it is necessary for them to work on their writing if they only want to learn to speak in the new language. However, I recommend that everyone make the effort to write regularly, even if only a little at a time. Writing is an excellent way to train yourself in the proper use of the language. You have the time to express yourself carefully when you write, whereas in conversation you are under greater pressure and need to be more spontaneous.

When you write, take the time to try to write correctly. Make a plan of what you are going to write. If you do not organize your thoughts ahead of time, you may not make sense writing in a foreign language. When correcting English I am always amazed at non-native speakers who just dash off emails and other texts without even using a spell-checker. Anyone working as a professional in an international company has to write correctly and understandably, otherwise it is the very image of the company that is damaged. If you are unable to do this for yourself, use the services of a text correcting service.

If you have trouble with verb tenses, think through the time when each action is taking place. Use the phrases you have mastered when you write, instead of simply translating from your native language. Many of the most common problems relating to word order, choice of words, prepositions, verb tenses and verb agreement can be eliminated by building your written language around the phrases you have learned.

Until you are fluent, try to speak the way you write and write the way you speak, in short, simple and complete sentences. Do not speak in a casual way and then try to write stilted or complicated prose. Even if native speakers are sloppy in their speech and use a lot of slang, as a learner you cannot afford to do so. You do not have a strong enough foundation in the new language. You will need to be aware of casual or slang speech in order to understand it. But you are best to avoid it until you are quite fluent and really sure when to use it. Even though it is hard work, writing is an excellent way to develop genuine eloquence in a new language.

If your speech is similar to your written style, each will reinforce the other. It is less stressful to accept corrections of what you write than to have your spoken language corrected, and it is easier to remember the written corrections. The corrections in your written work can then be applied to your spoken language. While spoken language is more forgiving than written language, the same phrases and words can be used effectively in both.

You should have your writing corrected regularly and your mistakes analyzed and measured. It is important to keep a statistical record of the kinds of errors you make most frequently. This enables you to concentrate on your major problems. You should then look for phrases in your reading that contain the kinds of errors you make most often, and save them to a database for regular review.

In the writing submitted for correction to The Linguist, the most common problems stem from improper use of vocabulary. It is not the rules of grammar that present the greatest difficulty, but rather the precise meaning of words and how they fit together with other words. To master the use of new vocabulary requires frequent exposure in different contexts. Learning whole phrases, rather than single words, will facilitate the learning of correct usage. Learning whole phrases will also help establish correct habits with regard to verb tenses, prepositions and other details of the language. The natural language that you read and listen to, if of good quality, can be a treasure chest of useful phrases. You need to be deliberate in searching them out and studying them, guided by the problems that are uncovered in your corrected writing.

Whoever corrects you writing should suggest new phrases to replace the incorrect ones. You should save these new phrases into your database and study them regularly. In this way writing can be tied back to the "engine" of language acquisition. The writing activity becomes like a quality control measure to ensure that you are acquiring the words and phrases that you will need. Each time you write and have your work corrected it is an opportunity to take a step closer to accurate expression in the new language.

It is worth considering the self-teaching methods of Heinrich Schliemann (1822-1890) the world-famous businessman turned archeologist who discovered the site of ancient Troy. As reported by Arnold Toynbee in *A Study of History* (Oxford University Press 1963), Schliemann was able to express his thoughts orally and in writing after about six weeks of self-study, in Modern Greek, Ancient Greek, Persian, Arabic, and Turkish. His method consisted of "reading a great deal aloud without making a translation, taking a lesson every day, constantly writing essays upon subjects of interest, correcting these under the supervision of a teacher, learning them by heart, and repeating in the next lesson what was corrected on the previous day." The motivated learner who is prepared to work every day can achieve great things. Fortunately, language learning is much easier today than it was in the 19th century.

When you receive a corrected version of something you have written, take the time to look at it. Read it aloud several times. Focus on the corrected phrases. Make them a part of your way of speaking in the new language. Especially if you do not have easy access to native speakers for conversation, this can be an inexpensive and yet intense learning activity. You can improve your vocabulary, sentence structure, pronunciation and general speaking skills. You can prepare yourself for what most people find the most enjoyable part of language learning: conversation with the native speaker.

Conversation

Your ultimate goal is to interact comfortably with native speakers. At an early stage you will want to try out what you have learned in order to build up your confidence and fluency. But conversation and speaking skills develop gradually and cannot be rushed. Do not be in a hurry or put pressure on yourself. Do not worry about how you sound, just focus on communicating. You will often feel that you are struggling, when in fact you are communicating quite successfully. The key to successful conversation is to try to relax and enjoy the experience. Focus on the meaning you are trying to communicate, not on how well you are doing. Do not think that your grammar and pronunciation are being judged, just try to get your meaning across. Your listeners want to understand you. When you are successful in communicating, give yourself a pat on the back.

You should seek every opportunity to speak with native speakers. Speaking with native speakers is the ultimate test of your ability. You can allow yourself to get caught up in the natural rhythm of the language. You will find that you naturally start to imitate certain ways of speaking of native speakers that you are in regular contact with. Do not expect native speakers to correct you, however, but just treat these opportunities for what they are, chances to communicate. Speaking with other foreign learners is useful as a means to practice what you have learned, but it does not provide the same opportunity for imitation and learning.

Aside from such non-structured opportunities to communicate in the language, it is also useful to arrange regular structured conversation sessions, where your pronunciation and language accuracy can be measured for feedback to you. This can be arranged with a private coach or teacher, or at a school.

Whenever you converse in the new language, use the phrases you know and build your conversation around these phrases. If possible you should make weekly lists of new words and phrases from your learning and deliberately try to use them. You will find that you can use your newly learned phrases as convenient components and build your conversation around them. Using them in conversation will also help you confirm that you really know how to use them.

You will need to make an effort to find people to talk with. If you live where the language is spoken, you may have friends or co-workers who are native speakers. You may be able to enroll in courses offered in the language you are learning, but on subjects other than the language itself. This and other activities can bring you into casual and friendly contact with native speakers who share your interests. If you do not have ready opportunities to meet native speakers, you will have to organize small groups of learners with or without native speaker coaches to meet and discuss subjects of common interest.

You can use the Internet to organize meetings at sites, such as at The Linguist Community section where there are conversation clubs on different subjects from books to current events. These encounters are for interaction, feedback and stimulus. They should be enjoyable and not stressful. They can vary from serious forums on politics, business or academic subjects, to more relaxed social exchanges. On The Linguis,t there will be formalized reports on both pronunciation and incorrect use of phrases that will be reported back to the users.

A formal language school can also offer excellent interaction and feedback, but one word of caution is necessary. Simply attending language school will not enable you to learn a language. Whether you are attending formal classes or not, you will do most of your learning on your own. You direct your own listening and reading activity. You work on learning and relearning words and phrases, you train yourself to pronounce correctly, and you work on your writing. When you choose the activity that suits your mood, your studies are more intense than when you are forced to follow the teacher's agenda.

Create Intensity

Learning a new language is most enjoyable when you are learning quickly, which requires intensity. In physical training you often hear the expression "no pain, no gain." Only intensely overworking certain muscles will bring about the increased strength and performance of those muscles. Casual exercise will not do more than maintain an existing level of fitness. The same is true of language training. Your goal should be constant improvement towards fluency, not just maintenance.

You need to overwork the language processing capability of your brain by constant and frequent repetition during a period of intense learning. This period may vary from three months to twelve months depending on your starting point and your goals. During this period you must maintain a sustained commitment to your task. Fluency cannot be attained without sweat forming on your brow. It can still be enjoyable, but just as in physical exercise, the methods of training must be efficient. In fact, the greater the efficiency of the training methods the more intense the learning experience, and therefore, the better the results.

The greatest intensity of learning is achieved when studying on your own, or when involved in communicating on a subject of interest with native speakers. Classrooms, especially with more than five people, are distracting and even a one-on-one class can be stressful if you are not in the mood. The more you can study on your own, the more you control what you are studying, and the more you follow your interests and inclinations, the faster you will learn. This does not mean that you do not need a teacher. In fact a teacher or coach is essential for feedback and for guidance. However, if you can maintain an intense program of self-study you may only need to meet with your teacher once or twice a week. A guided program of self-study is much less expensive and more effective than attending traditional language class. The condition is that you work intensively on your own.

Unfortunately most language learners are not sufficiently motivated to work hard intensely on their own, and that is why traditional language schools will continue to attract the majority of language students. I attribute my own success in language learning to my willingness to work very hard in an intense manner for specific periods of time to master new languages. All good language learners do this.

Schools have the advantage of forcing you to appear at certain times and requiring you to do specific assignments. Even when you do not learn, by attending class and doing your assignments you feel you have met a commitment and achieved something. The independent learning experience is different. It needs to be more intense, but it is not always clear what you have achieved.

That is why constant measurement can be so helpful. Measurement helps to create intensity. You need to measure how much time you have spent on different activities of the "engine" of language learning every day. How many hours did you repetitively listen to meaningful content every day? How many words did you read every day? How many words and phrases have you saved for learning? How many words do you know in total? As you record the significant effort you are putting into learning every day, you gain a sense of satisfaction and you are motivated to continue the level of intensity necessary for success.

Systems for self-learning, like The Linguist, will keep track of your input and output effort in terms of time spent, words and phrases learned, total words known, accuracy in writing and richness of vocabulary. This measurement helps you maintain the intensity needed to stay on course.

Set Clear Goals

To succeed in most activities you need to set goals. How much time are you willing to commit each day, and for how long? What skill level do you want to achieve? How many words do you know and how many do you want to know? How fluent do you want to be? Do you need to participate in business meetings in the new language? Do you need to follow university lectures? How close to native level do you want your pronunciation to be? Do you need to write business reports or school reports in the new language?

You may decide that you can commit to two hours per day for a period of six months or one hour a day for twelve months. This degree of commitment would mean a total of more than three hundred fifty hours and should produce a language breakthrough if the study methods are effective. During this period of concentration, you will have to sacrifice familiar activities in order to fulfill your commitment. If you develop the habit of listening at various times during the day, doing some casual reading, watching television, spending time in more dedicated study and having regular conversation sessions on subjects of interest, you can achieve the required level of intensity.

Even when working on your own, you will still need a teacher or language coach to provide feedback, help you diagnose your needs and adjust your goals. You should always measure your progress towards your goals. You must measure your input into the activities of the language acquisition "engine", listening, reading, and word and phrase study. You should measure your time spent on practicing output, pronunciation, writing and conversation. And finally you should measure the quality of the output.

But, in the end, you will be the one to know when you have reached your target. You will know how good your pronunciation is, or how comfortable you are in reading or expressing yourself. You will know when you are a linguist. You will then realize that you are never really satisfied with your level. You will continue to want to improve, but by pursuing your own interest in the language, the learning process will always be enjoyable and satisfying.

Invest in the Tools

If you are serious about learning the language, make sure you equip yourself with the necessary tools and learn how to use them. This initial investment is more important than spending time and money on additional language classes.

The time and money you have available for language learning is limited, so go out and buy reliable listening equipment to take with you wherever you go. The likelihood that you will put the required amount of time into listening increases with the portability of the listening device. Also, use good earphones. The effectiveness of listening increases significantly with good sound quality.

I own a portable CD player, a Minidisc player with a small microphone, a portable audio cassette player, and a small hand-held computer with a built-in MP3 player and microphone. With this equipment at my disposal, I am ready no matter what form the audio content comes in. I can buy cassette language systems and CD based audio books, download MP3 files, or record meetings, interviews and lectures for later listening. I can also record my own voice and upload files to a computer.

Choose what works for you. Decide how much you want to spend, and what the greatest source of your audio material will be. Language content from the Internet can be downloaded into MP3 players or MD players. Most new computers let you burn CDs. Most audio material you buy today is in CD or cassette form, but the quality and shelflife of CDs is better than cassettes and in language learning, sound quality is important. The MP3 player and MD player have the great advantage of being very small with high quality sound. But the choice is up to you.

To be a cost effective linguist today, you will need a personal computer and high speed Internet access. If you do not have this access at home you should identify a hub you can use for downloading and accessing content. This can be a library, your school, a friend or an Internet Café. Very often, this hub will offer instructions on how to access the content and how to download.

You will also need a good online or offline software dictionary, which gives you instant explanations in the language you are studying, as well as the all-important translation into your own language. Contrary to the view of some language teachers, I have always preferred to see the translation of a new word into my own language, rather than decipher an explanation in the language I was learning.

However, a dictionary can only provide you with a partial meaning of a new word. It will take time and significant exposure to the word in a natural context before you acquire a wider sense of the meaning of the word and the confidence to use it properly. You can also expect to forget whatever you look up in a dictionary pretty quickly. That is why it is so important to save all new words into lists, and preferably interactive lists such as is done at The Linguist. This makes it possible to regularly review these new words and phrases in conjunction with your reading and listening.

Before you decide where you are going to study a language, make sure you are equipped to succeed as an independent language learner! Now go to it!

A Final Word

In 2003, Mike Weir won the Masters Golf Tournament, probably the most prestigious golf tournament in the world. To defeat the world's best golfers required skill, determination and hard work over a long period of time. But above all it required an attitude. When Mike Weir was thirteen years old he wrote a letter to Jack Nicklaus, at that time the world's number one golfer. Mike, who was a left-handed golfer, asked Jack if he should continue left-handed, or try to switch to being right-handed, since almost all successful professional golfers were right-handed. Jack was gracious enough to reply, saying that Mike should stay left-handed; in other words, he should follow what was natural for him. (Zhuangzi, the Taoist philosopher who inspired our crooked tree logo, would have said the same!)

What impressed me about this story is Mike's commitment. He believed in himself and felt it quite appropriate to ask the world's greatest player (whom he did not know) to resolve an important question for him. He dared to write to the king of golf, and the king sent him an answer. Powered with that sort of attitude, Mike was able to overcome many obstacles and finally achieve greatness in his chosen field of endeavour.

You have read about the attitudes necessary for successful language learning. You have a description of effective techniques for acquiring language skills. You know what has to be done. Now it is up to you to believe in yourself and do it.

If you create the right habits, you will succeed. The rewards will more than compensate your efforts. Once you start learning languages you will not stop with just one.

Postscript: The long road

It is a long road that has no curves.
Doug Reid, Vice-President, Seaboard Lumber Sales, 1975

When I worked for Seaboard Lumber Sales in the late 1970s, one of my bosses was a man with an unlimited supply of witty sayings for every situation. When we faced difficulties he would say, "It is a long road that has no curves." I did not understand what he meant. Now I do. If you are on a long walk, it is much more interesting if there are some bends and changes in scenery. Similarly, the road to any achievement is made more interesting by the obstacles you must overcome. Life itself presents challenge after challenge. Facing these challenges is what makes life worth living. The road to building The Linguist language learning system was a long and winding one.

The idea to create a web site for language learning began in the summer of 2001 when I was working hard at learning Cantonese. Not only was I regularly listening to recordings of Cantonese on my minidisk recorder, but I would regularly tune in to the Cantonese radio stations in Vancouver. One day I heard a news story about a recent immigrant from China, a graduate in computer science from Tsing Hua University, who, upon arrival at the Vancouver airport, had had his life savings of roughly $7,000 stolen. Apparently, certain criminal groups knew that immigrants from China tend to bring relatively large sums with them in cash, and therefore target them.

At that time, in our company we were developing software systems for our lumber trading activities and for our house building activities. I thought that we might be able to employ this man. If he was good for our company we would gain a useful employee. If things did not work out, at least he would have some Canadian experience and some income to get him started in his new country. I found out where he lived and went to see him. He seemed like a sincere young man so I hired him.

It was obvious from the beginning that communication in English was a major problem, even though he had achieved a high score in TOEFL. It was a strain for him and for my employees. In addition, his background was more in hardware than in software, and he lacked the language skills to adapt to the different needs of our operation. He left amicably after eight months. He is now back in China, doing very well.

I found out from others that our case was not unique. The language barrier was a major problem, not only for the immigrants themselves, but for society as a whole. If these people could not find satisfactory employment and were forced to work for low wages at menial jobs, this delayed their integration into society.

I participated in a number of conferences on the integration of immigrants in the fall of 2001 and the spring of 2002, organized by various government-financed social welfare agencies that provided services to new immigrants. The general theme of these conferences was that government should do more. Government should provide more funding to these agencies. Government should subsidize employers to hire immigrants. Government should force professional associations to certify newcomers without requiring too much retraining or retesting to meet Canadian standards.

I felt that there was enough government money being spent on immigrant services without necessarily solving the problem. It did not seem to me that more government involvement was the solution. I heard criticism from immigrants who were not happy with the kind of English training programs already being offered. Some immigrants took government-sponsored language programs and did not make much of an effort to learn. Those who were motivated often could not afford to continue to go to school. They needed to work.

If a person wanted to learn English in a place like Vancouver, it should be possible to do so. I decided to create a language learning system that people could access from anywhere, at any time. Such a system should help them learn, if they were motivated. If we could develop a system that could help Vancouver immigrants, then we would have something that could be used anywhere in the world to teach any language. That was the birth of The Linguist.

It has been a long journey, unlike anything else I have done. I have had to start down many wrong roads only to have to give up and start again. I have spent a great deal of time and money and have learned a great deal.

My principle was always simple. I wanted to create audio and text content that people could access via the Internet and use to build up their language skills. I wanted to use modern technology to make it easier to learn and remember words and phrases, and to measure the learners' progress.

At first I hired a group of English teachers to write material of different levels of difficulty. The results were unsatisfactory. The content was artificial, childish and uninteresting. That is when we decided to use natural interviews with ordinary people as content. The reaction from our first pilot group was very positive. Our learners felt this material was unique, interesting and easy to learn from. I knew that there was other exciting content, like audio books, that needed to be made accessible to learners with our system.

The use of natural authentic content left us with the problem of grading this material to the level of the learner. We decided that we would have to devise a way of knowing each of the learners' vocabulary level. Then the system could grade the content for each learner. From that point, we realized that we needed an elaborate database to individually manage each learner's acquisition of words and phrases and to relate these words and phrases to the original language context. We also wanted to be able to test learners' writing and to link the writing back to the learning of phrases. Soon we had all kinds of ideas for our learning system. That was to become a problem. We had too many ideas.

The focus of our attention moved from the creation of content to the development of a learning system. There were many technical problems to overcome. I was unprepared for the difficulty of bringing this kind of functionality to the Internet. I was probably the worst culprit since I often came up with new ideas and demands on the programmers. It seemed that no deadline was ever met as the project increased in complexity.

My son, Mark, had been a part of the original team and had been instrumental in the design of our system. Having studied engineering at Yale, he had a more practical focus than I did, and often had to refuse to accommodate my constant suggestions of new features for our system. By the summer of 2003, he realized that we needed a new design for the website. We had problems with certain functions. He also felt that our website was not going to be robust enough to handle a high volume of users.

Together we analyzed what we had achieved and looked at what we had left to do. We realized that even people who want to learn a new language are often not sufficiently self-motivated to take advantage of our system. This required some changes in strategy. We needed to make it more fun.

We decided to redo the website yet again! We hired an advertising agency. They read the book and spent time on our site. Their conclusion was that the one outstanding characteristic of The Linguist was the simplification of the process of language learning. Furthermore, we all agreed that our main target group was professionally oriented internationally minded people between the ages of, roughly, 20 and 40. These people could come from any country in the world. Our site needed to be simple, practical and imply a sense of action to meet the tastes of our target group. Above all, the site needed to be clear and our users were telling us that it was not!

We looked again at the websites of our major competitors, companies who claimed to have hundreds of thousands and even millions of users. All of these sites were multi-coloured, busy, full of explanations and promotional text in an attempt to attract users. Some of these sites customized their websites to the tastes of different cultures.

We deliberately went a different route. We felt that The Linguist was not a website like the others. We were an integrated system that would help people learn languages fast and efficiently. We were not a game or fashion site. We reduced unnecessary explanations, unnecessary artistic effects, even unnecessary colour. We made the site as simple and straight forward as possible. We also made it as easy as possible. We felt that the design we chose was modern, yet culturally neutral, and therefore would work in every country.

The second point we accepted was that while our site was a fantastic resource for a very motivated and disciplined language learner, most users would benefit more from the site with the help of a native speaker coach or teacher. Even a small amount of individual personal interaction with a native speaker, as little as one hour a month, could make a great deal of difference in the motivation, and therefore, the eventual success of our users. We also needed to create a stronger sense of community amongst our learners. These are some of the challenges that lie before us.

I know that our adventure has only just begun. Many challenges remain. There are months and years of work ahead of us. It is satisfying to know that what we are doing can make a difference to peoples' lives, in their professional, cultural and social activities. We can help people achieve their goals and fulfill their potential. I look forward to getting to know the new linguists who will come forward to use our system in China and elsewhere in the world.

About the Author

Steve Kaufmann grew up in the English speaking part of Montreal, Quebec in the 1950s. Although he was taught French in school, he could not communicate in that language. It was only after he left high school that he became interested in learning French and was able to make himself fluent. This experience inspired a life-long interest in the discovery of languages and other cultures. After two years at Montreal's McGill University, Steve hitchhiked on a tramp freighter to get to Europe. He ended up studying in France while supporting himself at various odd jobs. He graduated from the elite Paris School of Political Science, l'Institut d'Etudes Politiques in 1966 and entered the Canadian Foreign Service.

As a Diplomat, Steve continued to immerse himself in the culture and languages of other countries. In preparation for the opening of diplomat relations with China, Steve was assigned to Hong Kong to learn Mandarin. During this time he made regular visits to China which was then at the height of the Cultural Revolution.

He next served at the Canadian Embassy in Japan, where he made himself fluent in Japanese, essentially by studying in his spare time. While at the Embassy, Steve was heavily involved in developing markets for Canadian forest products. In 1974 Steve left the Diplomatic Service to establish and manage Asian subsidiaries for two major Canadian forest products companies. In the early 1980s he returned to live in Vancouver. In 1987 he founded his own company which today has offices in Japan, Sweden and Canada, and of which he is the President and CEO.

Steve is fluent in French, Spanish, German, Italian, Mandarin, Cantonese, Japanese, Swedish and English and is working on two more, Korean and Portuguese. Steve I married with two sons and five grandchildren and lives in Vancouver, Canada.

In 2003, Steve decided to write of his experiences in exploring and discovering different cultures and languages in the hope that it would encourage more people to become "linguists".